METHOD
IN
SOCIAL
ANTHROPOLOGY

METHOD

IN

SOCIAL

ANTHROPOLOGY

Selected Essays by A. R. RADCLIFFE-BROWN

Edited by M. N. Srinivas

THE UNIVERSITY OF CHICAGO PRESS

CHICAGO & LONDON

The University of Chicago Press, Chicago 60637
The University of Chicago Press, Ltd., London

© 1958 by The University of Chicago
All rights reserved. Published 1958. Midway Reprint 1976
Printed in the United States of America

International Standard Book Number: 0-226-70220-0
Library of Congress Catalog Card Number: 58-11954

This is possibly the final volume of A. R. Radcliffe-Brown's published and unpublished contributions to social science in general and social anthropology in particular. It presents, in Part I, Radcliffe-Brown's major methodological papers in chronological order and follows, in Part II, with his last finished statement on the nature and development of social anthropology, originally prepared as the first portion of a projected introductory book on social anthropology. It is published with the kind permission and encouragement of Professor E. E. Evans-Pritchard, Radcliffe-Brown's literary executor, and any royalties will accrue to a research fund set up in Radcliffe-Brown's name.

We are greatly indebted to Professor M. N. Srinivas, the distinguished Indian social anthropologist, for the task of arranging and editing this volume and for his illuminating Introduction, in which he traces the development of Radcliffe-Brown's methodological and theoretical conceptions. Our thanks are also due the publishers of the *South African Journal of Science* and of *Nature*, and the officers of the British Association for the Advancement of Science and the Royal Anthropological Institute of Great Britain and Ireland, for permission to reprint the published essays included in this volume.

Professor Srinivas has also prepared a brief selective bibliography of books and essays concerned, in part at least, with Radcliffe-Brown's influence on anthropology. Already it is clear that it has been considerable, and it is still growing. This volume, we hope, will be a contribution to that end.

FRED EGGAN

TABLE OF CONTENTS

After his retirement from the chair of social anthropology at Oxford in July, 1946, Professor Radcliffe-Brown started working on an introductory book on social anthropology, a subject which he had taught with distinction in several universities in different parts of the world from Sydney to São Paulo. He managed to finish five chapters of the book by the end of 1950, and, unfortunately, that was as far as he got with it. Ill-health, frequent and long travel, teaching, and the many other calls on his time came in the way of his completing the book. In 1951 he gave the Huxley Memorial Lecture, "The Comparative Method in Social Anthropology" (included in this volume), and a year later he chose Australian cosmogony as the theme of his Josiah Mason lectures in the University of Birmingham; this was a subject which he had made his own and on which he used to lecture brilliantly. He then went to Grahamstown in South Africa, where he continued to teach social anthropology until serious ill-health made it impossible. He returned to England in 1955 and died on October 24, 1955.

As is well known, Radcliffe-Brown wrote with great care, handling words like precious stones. He usually wrote a piece several times before publishing it—the galley proofs of his famous work, *The Andaman Islanders*, were cut into sections and rearranged to make the argument clearer. His fastidiousness was partly responsible for his relatively meager output. His fragment on social anthropology, included in the present volume, illustrates Radcliffe-Brown's virtues as a writer: the style is very simple—in fact, deceptively so—clear, and singularly free from jargon. It provides a succinct and scholarly introduction to the subject.

It was thought that it would be a good idea to publish along with the chapters on social anthropology some of Radcliffe-Brown's papers on scope and method. These papers, written at different points in Radcliffe-Brown's professional career, have exercised much influence on the development of anthropological studies but have been published in journals and reports which are not easy to come by.[1]

Throughout his career as an anthropologist, Radcliffe-Brown was arguing for a rational division of the several subjects subsumed under the omnibus term "anthropology." The great stimulus given to anthropological studies by the theory of evolution has resulted in bringing together, within the framework of a single subject, several distinct disciplines, such as physical anthropology, ethnology, prehistoric archeology, linguistics, and social anthropology. Anthropology thus includes every aspect of primitive human life from technology to theology. Radcliffe-Brown considered such an arrangement not very rational, and he wanted a division of subjects on the basis of their logical affinity. He made this division in three of the essays included in this book: "Methods of Ethnology and Social Anthropology" (1923), "The Present Position of Anthropological Studies" (1931), and "Meaning and Scope of Social Anthropology" (1944). Chapter i of "Social Anthropology" is also concerned with this division.

In making these distinctions, Radcliffe-Brown was especially concerned with pointing out the differences be-

[1] It was decided to omit from this collection Radcliffe-Brown's "Some Problems of Bantu Sociology" (*Bantu Studies*, Nos. 1–3 [1921–22], pp. 38–46) and "Applied Anthropology" (presidential address to Section F of the Australian and New Zealand Association for the Advancement of Science, twentieth meeting, Brisbane, May–June, 1930).

tween social anthropology—the science of comparative sociology, which seeks universal laws governing human social behavior—and ethnology, which is a historical discipline interested in reconstructing the history of primitive peoples and in classifying their race and language. According to Radcliffe-Brown, ethnology ought to be studied in close collaboration with prehistoric archeology, while physical anthropology belongs to the biological sciences and ought to be studied as a part of the wider subject of human biology.

Radcliffe-Brown's ideas have been so successful that the distinctions he first advocated in 1923, in "The Methods of Ethnology and Social Anthropology," have become the commonplaces of British social anthropology today. But it is necessary to recall that in 1923 W. H. R. Rivers' reputation was still at its peak. In 1911, Rivers announced his conversion from the evolutionism of Morgan to a belief in the widespread character of diffusion and the necessity for ethnological analysis of culture; his ideas exercised a powerful influence during his life and for several years after his death. Rivers' ethnological approach and his marked bias for psychology were both threats to the growth, if not the existence, of the nascent discipline of social anthropology. Professor Lowie writes: "Medically and psychologically trained, Rivers did army service during the war, treating cases of shell-shock. His alert and suggestible mind was affected by the rise of psycho-analysis, and on that basis he attempted to ally psychology with ethnology. Whatever he may have added to psychological science in this way, he hardly advanced ethnology; to us at least, he does not seem to have done more than paraphrase ethnographic facts in psychiatric argot."[2]

In chapter ii of the fragment on social anthropology, Radcliffe-Brown traces briefly the history of the subject

[2] *The History of Ethnological Theory* (New York, 1937), p. 172.

over the last three centuries, and he makes it evident that many distinguished thinkers from several countries have contributed to its growth. It was Sir James Frazer, however, who first used the term "social anthropology" in the sense understood by British social anthropologists today. In 1908, in his inaugural lecture as the honorary professor of social anthropology in the University of Liverpool, he defined clearly the nature and scope of social anthropology. But that did not put a stop to pseudohistorical and psychological explanations for social facts and events. Radcliffe-Brown was the first English-speaking anthropologist to reject both these types of explanations and to argue that sociological facts demanded explanation in terms of sociological laws and not in terms of individual psychology or reconstructed history.

"The Methods of Ethnology and Social Anthropology" was published in 1923, a year after Rivers' death in 1922, and the latter year also saw the publication of two works of revolutionary import, Malinowski's *Argonauts of the Western Pacific* and Radcliffe-Brown's *Andaman Islanders*. The essay constitutes Radcliffe-Brown's earliest statement on the nature, scope, and affiliations of social anthropology, and his subsequent pronouncements do not reveal any radical departure from it. If any single essay can be called the charter—to use a favorite word of Malinowski—of modern British social anthropology, it is undoubtedly "The Methods of Ethnology and Social Anthropology." It was a charter of revolt when it first made its appearance.

It was in the course of his analysis of the ethnological approach that Radcliffe-Brown was led to distinguish between the different kinds of history practiced by his colleagues. He pointed out that ethnologists did not write "real" histories but conjectural histories which were at best probable and at worst mere piling-up of unverifiable guesses—which was, indeed, true of Rivers' *History of*

Melanesian Society (2 vols.; Cambridge: Cambridge University Press, 1914).

Radcliffe-Brown welcomed proper history where sufficient documentary material was available. He pointed out the value of history, though he took pains to emphasize that it was different from a "functional" or sociological explanation of the social institutions in question. In his own work he even reconstructed history. Professor Lowie, who is generally critical of Radcliffe-Brown's approach, points out that ". . . Radcliffe-Brown's theoretical intransigence on the subject of history wanes before data with which he is thoroughly familiar and, notwithstanding some qualms, he stoops to chronological hypotheses. The Yaralde kinship system 'cannot reasonably be supposed to have developed independently of these (Arande systems) . . . we must certainly assume some historical connection between them.' Again, 'the Kumbaingeri type is a stepping stone from the Kariera to the Arunta form.' Surely this is conjectural history."[3] Radcliffe-Brown also encouraged the historical interests of his students. Professors Lloyd Warner and Fred Eggan tell us: "We remember well his encouragement of our own early researches on historical contacts in northern Australia and on historical changes in the kinship systems of American Indian groups where documentary or other data were available to check historical influences."[4]

He also pointed out that the intensive field studies of social anthropologists resulted in valuable contributions to tribal and local history. But he did make a sharp distinction between historical and functional explanations. In the one, "explanation" consists in seeking out facts or events which have happened earlier and showing that the later facts or events arise out of the earlier. In the other,

[3] *Ibid.*, p. 226.

[4] Obituary notice on Radcliffe-Brown by F. Eggan and W. Lloyd Warner, *American Anthropologist*, LVIII, No. 3 (June, 1956), 544–47.

explanation consists in showing how one event or group of events is but one instance of a universal law. Knowledge of the history of an institution will help in discovering its social function, but the two are essentially different. "For social anthropology the task is to formulate and validate statements about the conditions of existence of social systems (laws of social statics) and the regularities which are observable in social change (laws of social dynamics)." The understanding of the development of human society (i.e., social evolution), however, "will be only in an integrated and organised study in which historical and sociological studies are combined."[5]

Attempts to "explain" complex social institutions by reference to "facts" of individual psychology were popular with British anthropologists up to the 1930's. But Radcliffe-Brown, following Durkheim, insisted that psychology and social anthropology deal with facts at different levels and that it is wrong to explain the social by reference to the individual. "I wish most emphatically to insist that social anthropology is a science just as independent of psychology as psychology itself is independent of physiology, or as chemistry is independent of physics; just as much and no more. This position is by no means novel. Durkheim and the important school of *L'Année Sociologique* have insisted upon it since 1895."[6] This does not mean, however, that Radcliffe-Brown ignored "human nature." He states, "One determining factor in the formation of human social systems is that basic human nature which it is the business of the general psychologist to study."[7]

It is necessary to remember that when an anthropologist is studying a tribe or village he is not studying "human nature with the lid off," as Aldous Huxley would

[5] "The Comparative Method in Social Anthropology."

[6] "The Methods of Ethnology and Social Anthropology."

[7] "Meaning and Scope of Social Anthropology."

say. The "lids" are there in every society, however primitive, and it is impossible to take them off. "When we study the 'psychology' of the French or the Germans or the people of the United States, we are dealing with those characteristics of mind or behaviour that result from 'conditioning' by a particular social system. Here the 'special' characteristics with which we are concerned are determined by the social system, while the social system itself is determined by the general characteristics of basic human nature."[8] Radcliffe-Brown's position on this point is largely accepted by British anthropologists today. In the United States, however, there is more traffic between anthropology and social psychology (especially that branch of it which is called "culture and personality") than there is in England. Anthropological studies in the United States are so organized that an undergraduate's time tends to be distributed more evenly than in England among the various disciplines subsumed under the term "anthropology"—physical anthropology, archeology, linguistics, ethnology, social anthropology, and "culture and personality." In the United States the distinctions between the various branches of anthropology are not drawn as sharply as in England, and social anthropology does not occupy as dominant a place. The term "cultural anthropology" is far more popular than "social anthropology" in the United States, and American anthropologists are more willing than their British colleagues to move from the social to the psychological, if not the biological, level.[9]

Again, in the United States anthropology and sociology form distinct clusters of studies, whereas in England social anthropology is recognized as a branch of sociology. It should not be surprising if the two subjects came

[8] *Ibid.*

[9] See the articles by G. P. Murdock and R. Firth on British social anthropology in the *American Anthropologist*, LIII (1951), 465–89.

even closer together in the near future. The different align-
ments of sociology and anthropology in the United States
and England are in some measure due to the greater
spread of Durkheim's and Radcliffe-Brown's ideas in
England.

Until 1931, Radcliffe-Brown described the subject matter of social anthropology as culture or social life. Subsequently, however, he used increasingly "social structure"
and "social system," and he began to drop the use of
"culture." This is seen clearly in his essay, "On the Concept of Function in Social Science."[10]

In 1937, at his Chicago Faculty Seminar, "A Natural
Science of Society," he went even further: "You cannot
have a science of culture. You can study culture only as a
characteristic of a social system. Therefore, if you are
going to have a science, it must be a science of social systems."[11] Subsequently, "social structure," which he regarded as a part of "social system," claimed his attention
more and more, and in 1940 he chose "social structure" as
the theme of his presidential address to the Royal Anthropological Institute.

It is worth recording, however, that he used the concept of "social structure" as early as 1914[12] in a course of
lectures he gave on social anthropology in Birmingham.
The concepts of "social structure" and "social integration" figure prominently in his address on applied anthropology to Section F of the Australian and New Zealand
Association for the Advancement of Science (twentieth
meeting, Brisbane, May–June, 1930). It was there that he

[10] It is based on the comments which Radcliffe-Brown made on a
paper read by Dr. A. Lesser to the American Anthropological Association in 1935. Reprinted in *Structure and Function in Primitive
Society* (London, 1952), chap. x.

[11] See *A Natural Science of Society* (Glencoe, Ill.: Free Press,
1957), p. 106.

[12] See Professor Fortes' memoir on Radcliffe-Brown in *Man*,
LVI (November, 1956), 149–53.

stated what he considered "one of the most important laws of social integration viz:—, the 'law of opposition.'" The "law" formulated by Radcliffe-Brown is that "in any segmentary organization the unity and solidarity of a group or segment depends upon the existence of some form of social opposition, i.e., some form of socially regulated and organised antagonism, between it and the other groups or segments with which it is in contact, which opposition serves to keep the separate segments differentiated and distinct. Opposition, which I am here using as a technical term for socialised or institutionalised antagonism, may take many different forms, and warfare is only one of them."[13]

Since 1940 the concept of social structure has provided the chief theoretical framework for British social anthropology. In the United States, a distinction is often made between "functionalists" and "structuralists," the former being the followers of Malinowski and the latter the followers of Radcliffe-Brown. This distinction is too neat, but it highlights an important fact: in contemporary British social anthropology, structure has largely replaced culture. It is not unlikely, however, that this present preoccupation with social structure may itself lead, in the not distant future, to a systematic examination of the relation between structure and culture on a comparative basis.

Included in this volume is the abstract of a paper directly bearing on applied anthropology which Radcliffe-Brown read before the Fourth Panpacific Science Congress at Java in 1929.[14] This interest in applied anthropology is also evident—in fact, too much so—in his paper, "Some Problems of Bantu Sociology" (*Bantu Studies*, Nos. 1–3 [1921–22]). He emphasized the utility of social anthropology to colonial administrators, and one of the

[13] *Ibid.*, p. 272.
[14] "Historical and Functional Interpretations of Culture in Relation to the Practical Application of Anthropology to the Control of Native Peoples."

criticisms he made of ethnology was that it had no "practical" use. In his desire to popularize social anthropology, Radcliffe-Brown was seeking the help of those interested in good government in the British colonies.

However, faith in applied anthropology is also a logical consequence of Radcliffe-Brown's central assumption that social anthropology is a science like physics, chemistry, and biology. One of Radcliffe-Brown's aims was to try to apply the logic of the natural sciences rigorously to social anthropology. This led him to the conclusion that, just as in the other natural sciences, in social anthropology the "pure" scientists discover universal laws which the "applied" scientists use for the welfare of mankind. The effectiveness of applied anthropology has increased as progress continues in pure anthropology, while the neglect of pure science in the long run injures applied science.

Besides, we should not forget that Radcliffe-Brown grew up in Victorian England, which was marked by faith in reason and in progress, which is the result of the application of reason to human affairs. This faith drew strength from Radcliffe-Brown's own studies in the Positivist springs of French sociology.[15]

Radcliffe-Brown used to tell his friends and colleagues that Prince Peter Kropotkin was his neighbor in Birmingham and that during his vacations from Cambridge (where he was known as "Anarchy Brown") he used to visit the great Anarchist philosopher. On these occasions they discussed everything, including Radcliffe-Brown's panaceas for what he regarded as the ills of contemporary England. Kropotkin pointed out to the young reformer that it was necessary to study and understand society before trying to change it and that in order to understand

[15] It may be recalled here that Durkheim, from whom Radcliffe-Brown took so much, wrote a book on socialism, and that Juárez, the Mexican revolutionary, was a classmate of Durkheim.

such a complex society as Victorian England one should begin by making a systematic study of a faraway primitive community.

When Radcliffe-Brown felt that social anthropology had become established as a subject in British universities, his keenness for applied anthropology was tempered by his concern for making advances in pure social anthropology. He wrote in 1944: "The demand on social anthropologists to spend too much of their time on practical problems would inevitably reduce the amount of work that can be given to the development of the theoretical side of the science. But without a sound basis in theory, applied anthropology must deteriorate and become not applied science, but merely empirical research."[16]

Throughout his academic career, Radcliffe-Brown stressed the importance of the comparative method. In fact, according to him, one of the crucial distinctions between social anthropology and sociology consisted in the use of the comparative method by the former and its neglect by the latter. Radcliffe-Brown was even willing to call social anthropology "sociology" as long as the prefix "comparative" was added. This insistence on the comparative method was not merely at the level of doctrine. He practiced it all the time. As is well known, he published an extremely valuable comparative study of the social organizations of Australian tribes in 1931.[17] The subject of his Huxley Memorial Lecture was the comparative method in social anthropology; in the lecture he proceeded from a consideration of an Australian folktale to the role of institutionalized opposition in social structure.

I hope that this collection of essays and addresses of Professor Radcliffe-Brown in a single volume will be useful to students of the subject as well as to professional social anthropologists. I am grateful to Professor Evans-

[16] "Meaning and Scope of Social Anthropology."
[17] "Oceania Monographs," No. 1 (Melbourne, 1931).

Pritchard, literary executor for Professor Radcliffe-Brown, for permission to publish the essays included in this book. In deference to Professor Evans-Pritchard's wishes, the profits of this book will be set apart as a special fund to help students of anthropology. I am indebted to Professors Sol Tax and Fred Eggan for help and encouragement in the planning of this book and for seeing it through the press, and to Professor D. G. Mandelbaum for help and advice.

M. N. SRINIVAS

Department of Sociology
Maharaja Sayajirao University of
Baroda, India

A Select Chronological Bibliography of Books and Essays Dealing with A. R. Radcliffe-Brown's Influence on Anthropology

LOWIE, R. H. *The History of Ethnological Theory*. New York: Farrar & Rinehart, Inc., 1937, pp. 221–29.

EGGAN, F. (ed.). *Social Anthropology of North American Tribes*. Chicago: University of Chicago Press, 1937. (See especially ROBERT REDFIELD's Introduction for the influence Radcliffe-Brown exerted on American anthropology in the thirties. The second edition (1955) includes additional essays by SOL TAX and FRED EGGAN which are helpful in estimating Radcliffe-Brown's influence.)

FORTES, M. (ed.). *Social Structure: Studies Presented to Radcliffe-Brown*. Oxford: Clarendon Press, 1949.

EVANS-PRITCHARD, E. E. *Social Anthropology*. London: Cohen & West, 1951.

MURDOCK, G. P. "British Social Anthropology," and FIRTH, R. "Contemporary British Social Anthropology," *American Anthropologist*, LIII (1951), 465–89.

FORTES, M. *Social Anthropology at Cambridge since 1900*. (Inaugural lecture.) Cambridge: Cambridge University Press, 1953.

————. "Radcliffe-Brown's Contributions to the Study of Social Organization," *British Journal of Sociology*, Vol. VI, No. 1 (March, 1955).

————. Obituary note on Radcliffe-Brown in *Man*, LVI (November, 1956), 149–53.

ELKIN, A. P. Obituary note on Radcliffe-Brown in *Oceania*, XXVI (June, 1956), 239–51.

EGGAN, F., and WARNER, W. LLOYD. Obituary note on Radcliffe-Brown in *American Anthropologist*, LVIII, No. 3 (June, 1956), 544–47.

FIRTH, R. "Alfred Reginald Radcliffe-Brown 1881–1955," *Proceedings of the British Academy*, Vol. XLII. London: Oxford University Press, 1957.

PART I

ESSAYS ON SCOPE
AND METHOD

Chapter I

THE METHODS OF ETHNOLOGY AND SOCIAL ANTHROPOLOGY[1]

In this address I cannot, I think, do better than deal with a subject which has for some years occupied, and is still occupying, the minds of ethnologists and anthropologists all over the world, namely that of the proper aims and methods to be followed in the study of the customs and institutions of uncivilized peoples. The subject is very obviously one of fundamental importance, for a science is hardly likely to make satisfactory progress, or to obtain general recognition, until there is some agreement as to the aims which it should pursue and the methods by which it should seek to attain those aims. But in spite of the many books and papers that have been devoted to the question of method in the past ten or fifteen years, agreement has not yet been reached. The subject is still open for discussion, is still, indeed, a burning one, and we cannot do better, I think, than open our proceedings by considering it.

The names ethnology and social or cultural anthropology have been applied without any constant discrimination to the study of culture or civilization, which, according to the definition of Tylor, is "that complex whole which includes knowledge, belief, art, morals, law, custom, and any other capabilities and habits acquired by

[1] *South African Journal of Science*, XX (October, 1923), 124–47. Presidential address to Section E, South African Association for the Advancement of Science, July 13, 1923.

3

man as a member of society." Such being the subject matter of the study the question of method which arises is how we are to study the facts of culture, what methods of explanation we are to apply to them, and what results of theoretical interest or practical value we are to expect from our study.

Tylor himself, whose right to the title of the father of the science I think no one will dispute, pointed out that there are two different methods by which the facts of culture may be explained,[2] and I believe that the confusion that has arisen in the science is in some large part due to the failure to keep these two methods carefully separated.

Let us see what these two methods of explanation are. There is first what I propose to call the historical method, which explains a given institution or complex of institutions by tracing the stages of its development, and finding wherever possible the particular cause or occasion of each change that has taken place. If, for instance, we are interested in representative government in England, we may study its history, noting the changes that have taken place from the earliest times, and thus tracing the development down to the present. Wherever we have adequate historical data we may study the facts of culture in this way.

The important thing to note about explanations of this type is that they do not give us general laws such as are sought by the inductive sciences. A particular element or condition of culture is explained as having had its origin in some other, and this in turn is traced back to a third, and so on as far back as we can go. In other words, the method proceeds by demonstrating actual temporal relations between particular institutions or events or states of civilization.

Now with regard to the institutions of uncivilized peoples we have almost no historical data. If, for instance, we are interested in the customs of the native

[2] Researches into the Early History of Mankind, page 5.

tribes of Central Australia, it is obvious at once that we can never obtain any direct information as to the history of these tribes. In such instances, therefore, the only possible way to apply the historical method of explanation is by making, on the basis of whatever evidence of an indirect kind we can find, a hypothetical reconstruction of the past history of these tribes.

A great deal of what is generally called ethnology has consisted of such theoretical or conjectural history. Let me illustrate the method by reference to a specific example. Off the east coast of this continent there lies a large island—Madagascar. A first examination of the people of the island shows that they are in some ways related, as we should expect, to the peoples of Africa. You may find, particularly on the western side, many individuals of distinctly negro, *i.e.*, African type, in respect, I mean, of their physical characters. And quite a number of the elements of Madagascar culture seem to be African also. But a closer examination shows that there are elements both of race and culture that are not African, and a study of these enables us to demonstrate without question that some of them have been derived from southeastern Asia. A consideration of the racial and cultural features of Madagascar as they exist at the present time enables us to say with practical certainty that, at a period of time not many centuries ago, there was an immigration into the island of people from Asia who were related in language, in culture, and at least to some extent in race, to the present inhabitants of the Malay Archipelago. We can even fix dates, rather vague, it is true, between which this migration took place. It must have been earlier than our first historical accounts of Madagascar, and it must have been later than the introduction of iron-working into the region from which the immigrants came.

A more detailed study of the racial and cultural features of Madagascar would enable us to reconstruct a good deal more of the history of the island. We see that there are at least two elements that have been combined in the culture of the island, two culture-strata as they are sometimes, not very appropriately, called, and a thorough systematic examination of the culture in comparison with the cultures of S.E. Asia and of Africa would permit us to analyse the existing complex of culture traits, so that we could say of many of them whether they were brought by the immigrants or whether they belonged to the earlier population of the island. And in this way we should be able to reconstruct some of the characters of the culture that existed in the island before the invasion.

In this way we explain the culture of Madagascar by tracing out the historical process of which it is the final result, and in default of any historical records we do this by means of a hypothetical reconstruction of the history based on as complete a study as possible of the racial characters, the language and the culture of the island at the present time, supplemented, if possible, by the information given by archaeology. In our final reconstruction some things will be quite certain, others can be established with a greater or less degree of probability, and in some matters we may never be able to get beyond mere guessing.

You will see from this example that we are able to apply the method of historical explanation even where we have no historical records. From written documents we can only learn the history of civilization in its most advanced stages during the last few centuries, a mere fragment of the whole life of mankind on earth. Archaeologists, turning over the soil, and laying bare the buildings or dwelling sites, and restoring to us the implements, and occasionally the bones, of races and peoples of long ago, enable us to fill in some of the details of the vast prehistoric period. The ethnological analysis of culture, which I have illustrated by the example of Madagascar, supplements the knowledge derived from history and archaeology.

This historical study of culture gives us only a knowledge of events and of their order of succession. There is another kind of study which I propose to speak of as "inductive," because in its aims and methods it is essentially similar to the natural or inductive sciences. The postulate of the inductive method is that all phenomena are subject to natural law, and that consequently it is possible, by the application of certain logical methods, to discover and prove certain general laws, *i.e.*, certain general statements or formulae, of greater or less degree of generality, each of which applies to a certain range of facts or events. The essence of induction is generalisation; a particular fact is explained by being shown to be an example of a general rule. The fall of the apple from the tree and the motions of the planets round the sun are shown to be different examples of the law of gravitation.

Inductive science has conquered one realm of nature after another: first the movements of the stars and planets and the physical phenomena of the world around us; then the chemical reactions of the substances of which our universe is composed; later came the biological sciences which aim at discovering the general laws that govern the reactions of living matter; and in the last century the same inductive methods have been applied to the operations of the human mind. It has remained for our own time to apply these methods to the phenomena of culture or civilization, to law, morals, art, language, and social institutions of every kind.

There are then, these two quite different methods of dealing with the facts of culture, and, since they are different, both in the results they seek, and in the logical methods by which they strive to attain those results, it is advisable to regard them as separate, though doubtless connected, studies, and to give them different names.

Now the names ethnology and social anthropology seem to be very suitable for this purpose, and I propose to devote them to it. There is already noticeable, I think, a distinct tendency to differentiate the use of the two terms in very much this way, but it has never, so far as I am aware, been carried out systematically. I would propose then, to confine the use of the term ethnology to the study of culture by the method of historical reconstruction described above, and to use the term social anthropology as the name of the study that seeks to formulate the general laws that underlie the phenomena of culture.[3] In making this suggestion I am doing nothing more, I think, than make explicit a distinction that is already implicit in a great deal of the current usage of the terms.

I think that the clear recognition of the existence of two quite different methods of dealing with the facts of culture will help us to understand the controversies on method that have been occupying the attention of students in recent years.

During the second half of the last century the conception of evolution was occupying, or even dominating, the minds of scientists, and the anthropologists of that time were therefore very largely compelled to take up the evolutionary point of view in their study of culture. Now the notion of evolution is open to ambiguity. If we look at it from the inductive point of view a process of evolution is one produced by the cumulative action of a single cause or a number of causes acting continuously. Thus biological evolution, according to the Darwinian theory, is a process due to the continuous action of the principles of

[3] It may be asked why I do not use the word "sociology" instead of the decidedly more cumbersome "social anthropology." Usage must count for something, and a good deal of what is commonly called sociology in English-speaking countries is a somewhat formless study of whose votaries Steinmetz says "on désire des vérités larges, éternelles, valables pour toute l'humanité, comme prix de quelques heures de spéculation somnolente."

heredity, variation, and natural selection. In this sense the development of culture can only be shown to be a process of evolution by demonstrating certain specific principles or laws, from the continued action of which it has resulted. But if we adopt what might be called the historical point of view a process of evolution may sometimes be regarded as a series of successive stages of development. Thus, in the history of living matter on the earth the evidence of geology shows us that there have been successive periods characterised by the appearance of different forms of living organisms, from the invertebrates to the higher mammals. But these successive stages are only really understood when we have formulated the laws by which they have been produced; and only then can they be regarded as stages of a process of evolution.

It was almost entirely from the historical and not from the inductive point of view that the anthropologists of the last century considered evolution, and their aim was therefore not to discover fundamental laws operating in the development of culture, but to show that that development had been a process by which human society passed through a number of stages or phases. This is abundantly evident when we remember a few of the topics of discussion with which anthropology was largely concerned until a few years ago. There was, for instance, the view, first expressed by Bachofen, that every human society passes through a matriarchal stage, *i.e.*, a stage of development in which kinship is counted only or chiefly through females, through the mother and not through the father, with the corollary that matrilineal peoples are everywhere more primitive than patrilineal peoples, *i.e.*, represent an earlier stage of development or evolution. Then, when interest in totemism was aroused, some anthropologists, basing their conclusions on the very wide distribution of the institution among uncivilized peoples, supposed that totemism was a necessary stage in the development of society and religion; and Kohler, and following him, Durkheim, even went so far as to suppose that the totemic form of society was the very earliest stage in the development of society about which we can obtain information.

The best example of the kind of theories which were the chief concern of what has been called the evolutionary school of anthropology is to be found in Lewis Morgan's "Ancient Society." There he attempts to define a number of stages of social development, each characterised by certain social institutions; and he regards the savages of the present day as representing the stages through which civilized peoples passed centuries ago. Morgan's theories were not accepted in their entirety by other anthropologists, but some of them were, and still are, accepted by a number of students of the subject. And even those who rejected Morgan's particular hypotheses at any rate accepted his general point of view, the so-called, and I think miscalled, "evolutionary" standpoint.

The assumption that Morgan and other anthropologists made was that the development of culture has been unilinear; all the various cultures of which we have knowledge can be arranged in a single series in one line, so that any culture high up in the series may be assumed to have passed through stages which are represented by those lower in the series. This assumption, still apparently accepted by some, has become more and more difficult to defend as our knowledge of the peoples of the earth and the diversity of their culture has increased. An overwhelming body of facts shows us that the development of culture has not been unilinear, but that each society develops its own special type as the result of its history and its environment.

However, I have not time, on this occasion, to enter on a criticism of the so-called evolutionary school. It has been subjected to very extensive criticism in recent years, in England, in Germany, and in America, and I may refer you to the book by Professor Lowie entitled "Primitive Society" for a reasoned and, I think, conclusive criticism of the type of evolutionary theory of which Morgan is the most typical representative. All that I am concerned with here is to point out that the anthropologists of this school considered culture and the history of culture from one standpoint only, namely, as a process of development, and were interested only or chiefly in problems of development, and that they regarded the development of culture from the historical standpoint as a succession of stages rather than from the inductive standpoint as the result of the action of specific laws. To come to the heart of the matter, as I see it, the evolutionary anthropology was never quite sure of its own aims, never definitely decided whether it was seeking to make a reconstruction of the history of culture, or to discover the general laws of culture as a whole. The result of this lack of certainty was a fundamental vice of method which I have no time now to deal with, but which I shall have to mention again later in this address.

Already, in the last century, there was an important school in Germany which adopted principles of method fundamentally different from those of the evolutionary school. This school, which was founded by Ratzel, was sometimes called the "geographical" school. Of its latest representatives, Schmidt calls his method "kulturhistorische" and Frobenius speaks of "Kulturmorphologie," while Graebner and others speak of their studies as ethnology. The chief feature of the school is that they concentrate their attention, sometimes exclusively, on the phenomena of the diffusion of culture. We know that elements of culture may be transferred from one region to another, or from one people to another, by various processes. Thus, in recent times, Japan has adopted many of the elements of European civilization. This process, which we can watch going on around us, is evidently nothing new but has been going on since mankind first spread over the earth, and it is fairly evident that it must have played a very important part in the history of culture.

In the early years of this century the study of culture had thus reached a position in which there were two different schools, following divergent aims, and having little or no connection with one another. The evolutionary anthropologists looked at everything from the point of view of development, and tended to look upon the development of culture as a process of unilinear evolution. The students of "culture-history" studied almost exclusively phenomena of the transfer of culture elements from one region to another, and either rejected or were not interested in the notion of evolution. The first of these two schools was more prominent in England, and the second in Germany.

In 1911 Dr. Rivers, in his Presidential Address to the Anthropological Section of the British Association, drew attention to this divergence between the methods of work of the evolutionary anthropologists and the students of culture-history, and suggested that the two methods must be combined if the study of culture is to progress. He expressed the view that before we can consider problems of development we must consider the effects of diffusion. "Evolutionary speculations can have no firm basis unless there has been a preceding analysis of the cultures and civilizations now spread over the earth's surface."

What Dr. Rivers calls the "ethnological analysis of culture," which I have already illustrated from the example of Madagascar, thus came into greater prominence in England, largely through the influence of Rivers himself, and though he has been lost to us by an untimely death that has been one of the greatest losses to the science in recent years, there are in England writers such as Perry and Elliott Smith who are enthusiastically and energetically pursuing studies along these lines.

I have no time to deal with the theories and methods of these writers, and all that I am now concerned with is to show you how under their influence the definitely historical point of view is coming more and more to be adopted. The older anthropologists, as I have remarked, were not quite sure whether they wished to reconstruct the history of civilization or to discover its laws, and often tried to do the two things at once. The newer writers are quite sure of their aim, which is to show how different elements of culture have been carried over the world by diffusion from a single centre. Their method is therefore the historical one.

In America, after the important work of Morgan, there was comparatively little theoretical work. Students of culture were fully occupied in collecting information about the rapidly disappearing natives of their country, and setting an example to the rest of the world which has unfortunately not been followed, at any rate, by the British Empire. But in the last ten years the question of the explanation of the great mass of data that has been thus collected has received increasing attention, and the tendency has been to adopt very definitely what I have called the historical method of explanation. The influence of Boas has been strongly in this direction. A very definite insistence on the strictly limited historical point of view is to be found in the paper entitled "Eighteen Professions," published in 1915 by Professor Kroeber. The evolutionary doctrines, particularly those represented by Morgan, have been subjected to extensive criticism by many writers, of whom I may mention Swanton and Lowie. A single quotation will suffice to illustrate the point of view that is on the whole typical of American writers of the present day, or at any rate of a large number of them, and I will take this from a work in which Sapir endeavours to lay down the principles by which it is possible to reconstruct the history of culture from a study of the local distribution of different culture elements. Under the heading "Ethnology as an Historical Science" he writes:

Cultural anthropology is more and more rapidly getting to realise itself as a strictly historical science. Its data can not be understood, either in themselves, or in their relation to one another, except as the end-points of specific sequences of events reaching back into the remote past. Some of us may be more interested in the psychological laws of human development that we believe ourselves capable of extracting from the raw material of ethnology and archaeology, than in the establishment of definite historical facts and relationships that would tend to make this material intelligible, but it is not at all clear that the formulation of such laws is any more the business of the anthropologist than of the historian in the customarily narrow sense of the word.

Sapir uses the words ethnology and anthropology as being interchangeable, but he is speaking of the study that I am proposing to call distinctively ethnology, and he is thus of opinion that it should limit itself strictly to the historical method of interpretation and exclude all attempts to discover general laws.

Thus we see that out of the undifferentiated or scarcely differentiated ethnology-anthropology of the last century there has gradually been marked off a special science (to which I propose to restrict the name ethnology) which is limiting itself more and more strictly to the historical point of view. The majority of its students reject the evolutionary theories of earlier days, either absolutely or at any rate as unproved and requiring modification. Some of them confine themselves almost entirely to problems of the diffusion of culture, while others deal also with problems of development, but only from the limited point of view to which they have been led by their recognition of ethnology as a systematic attempt to reconstruct the history of culture.

Efforts are being made to define as precisely as possible the methods of this study. The subject has been dealt with by Graebner in Germany, by Rivers in England, and by several writers in America. Unfortunately, these various writers have not been able, up to the present, to come to any general agreement as to the methods that ethnology should follow. In particular, there is very wide disagreement on some of the methodological assumptions and on questions of what does and what does not constitute evidence. Thus some ethnologists, of whom Elliott Smith is perhaps the most extreme example, tend to explain all similarities of culture all over the world as being due to diffusion from a common centre. If they find the same element of culture in two regions, whether they be related regions or not, they assume that this has been carried from a single centre. They would, as a general rule, deny the possibility of the same invention being made twice, or of the same institution being developed independently in different places at different times. I believe that Elliott Smith would even regard all the various forms of totemism as having had a single origin and spread from a single centre. On the other side, there are some who consider it quite possible for the same invention to be made twice and for similar institutions to be developed in societies having no direct or indirect contact with each other. Thus, some of the American writers hold that it is at least possible that pottery may have been independently discovered at least twice, in the Old World and in the New. As long as there is this disagreement about the fundamental methodological postulates of the study it is obvious that there can be no general agreement as to results. The evidence adduced by some writers in support of their theories is rejected by others as being no evidence, and instead of co-operation we get controversy, which raises passions, confuses issues, and poisons that atmosphere of calm impartiality in which alone science can live. We can only hope that the ethnologists, having come to a recognition of the limited character of their study as an attempt to reconstruct the history of culture, may be able to reach a larger measure of agreement as to methods and so to give us results that may be presented to the world at large as having behind them the authoritative acceptance of the whole body of workers in the subject.

But what of the other kind of study that was at first included in the anthropology-ethnology complex? We have seen that such writers as Kroeber and Sapir insist on the need of excluding from their particular science (ethnology as I am calling it) all attempts to discover general laws. They would not, I suppose, deny that it is possible to discover general laws in the phenomena of culture, or that the attempt to do so is justifiable. They would admit, I suppose, that it is possible to study the facts of culture from the inductive point of view, according to the same methods that the natural sciences apply to all the other phenomena of the universe. But both the two writers mentioned, and others also, commonly refer to such inductive study of culture as "psychology."

I wish most emphatically to insist that social anthropology is a science just as independent of psychology as psychology itself is independent of physiology, or as chemistry is independent of physics; just as much and no more. This position is by no means novel. Durkheim and the important school of the *Année Sociologique* have insisted upon it since 1895.

I cannot on this occasion discuss the matter of the relation of social anthropology to psychology, but I will attempt to make clear the difference between them by an example. A man commits a murder; the police arrest him; he is brought before a judge and jury and tried; and is hanged by the hangman. Here we have a situation in which a number of individuals with their own thoughts, feelings, and actions, are concerned. It is possible to study the behaviour of these individuals, the murderer, the policeman, the judge, etc., within the general situation, which we should have to take for granted. Such a study would be essentially a matter for psychology. But that study, however far we carried it, would not provide us with any explanation of the whole procedure in which the individuals play their respective parts. For this purpose we must study the situation as a whole, considering it as an action carried out by the society, the State, through its specially appointed representatives, as a collective reaction on the part of the society to the particular circumstances resulting from the murder. And then the individuals as particular persons, with their particular thoughts and feelings, become of no interest or importance for our purpose. The object of our study is the process as a whole and the individuals do not concern us except in so far as they necessarily enter into that process. Now such studies of social institutions and social reactions are the special task of social anthropology, as I defined it at the beginning of this address.

The distinction between psychology and social anthropology may therefore be stated, somewhat roughly, by saying that the former deals with individual behaviour in its relation to the individual; the latter deals with the behaviour of groups or collective bodies of individuals in its relation to the group. It is quite true that collective behaviour involves the actions of individuals. We have seen that the process by which a society inflicts punishment on a murderer involves actions by the policeman, the judge, and the hangman; and if we were considering the matter fully we should have to add the journalist who reports the trial and the citizen who reads the report in his newspaper. But the example has shown us that psychology and social anthropology look at these actions from quite different points of view. What, in them, is relevant to one science is largely irrelevant to the other.

I cannot hope, in the time available on this occasion, to show you exactly what are the differences between psychology and social anthropology. But perhaps the example I have chosen is sufficient to show you that there is a difference. Now, I think that one of the chief reasons for the failure of social anthropology to establish itself in the position it ought to occupy has been the failure to recognize that it is quite distinct from psychology. The study called "folk-psychology" in Germany, and a great deal of anthropology in England, have consisted of attempts to explain the customs and beliefs of primitive peoples in terms of psychology, *i.e.*, of the mental processes of the individual. The belief in magic, for example, is explained as a result of the psychological laws of the association of ideas. Such applications of psychology to the phenomena of culture can never make a science, any more than an attempt to explain the behaviour of the individual entirely in terms of physiology can give us an adequate substitute for psychology. If this were all that social anthropology could offer, then those writers, who include under psychology all study of culture that is not strictly historical, would be justified. But once we recognise, as it is full time that we did recognise, that social anthropology is an independent science, with its own special subject matter, its own distinctive methods, aiming at the discovery of laws that are in no sense laws of psychology, then and only then will it find its proper place and make progress.

A second thing that has stood in the way of the development of social anthropology has been the influence of the idea of evolution in the particular form in which it was first developed, with the historical bias which from the beginning has been noticeable in the study of culture. We have seen that modern ethnology has been led to reject the notion of evolution as a succession of phases through which human society passes. It is equally necessary for social anthropology to reject the evolutionary doctrine in this form as being, at any rate, entirely unproved.

If social anthropology is to use the idea of evolution at all (and for myself I think it can and should do so) it must be in the form of a statement of general laws or principles from the continuous action of which the various past and present forms of society have resulted (in just the same way as the evolutionary theory of biology attempts to state the general laws of which the action has produced the various living and extinct species). But such laws cannot be stated adequately until the science has already made considerable progress.

The effect of the historical bias of the early anthropology, and of the false idea of evolution to which it led such writers as Morgan, was to set anthropologists seeking, not for laws, but for origins. We have had theories of the origin of totemism, of the origin of exogamy, and even theories of the origin of language, of religion, and of society itself; and theories of this kind have occupied a very large place in the literature of anthropology. But it is open to doubt whether they have really advanced our knowledge and understanding of civilisation, except in a very indirect way by calling attention to the interest of the culture of primitive peoples and thus leading to their fuller study.

Let me illustrate the difference between the study of origins and the study of laws by a specific example. We have had in the last half century a large number of theories of the origin of totemism, none of which has yet obtained, or seems likely to obtain, general acceptance. Perhaps the best known is that of Sir James Frazer, according to which primitive man, being ignorant of the physiology of conception, concluded that a woman was impregnated by the food she ate; on the basis of this belief there arose customs by which each individual was required to observe certain ritual obligations to the species of animal or plant from which he had, as it were, sprung; in this way arose one form of totemism (conceptional totemism) and from this all others are derived. Sir James Frazer does not tell us whether he thinks that this process took place once in a certain region and that from that centre totemism was spread over the world, or that the same process has taken place independently in different parts of the world.

The methodological objection to this theory, and to all theories of the same type, is that there seems no possible way of verifying them. We may be able to show that totemism might have arisen in this way (although that involves a large number of assumptions as to how social institutions do arise), but we are unable, by any means that I can imagine, to prove that this is the way in which it actually did arise.

Moreover, the theory, and others like it, even if it explains how totemism at one time came into existence, does not explain how it succeeds in continuing in existence. And that is a problem quite as important as the problem of origin.

Now if we leave aside altogether the question of the possible origin or origins of totemism, and try instead to discover its laws, we reach a theory of an entirely different kind, and if you will permit me I will illustrate the matter by a brief statement of my own theory of totemism, in the form of a few general statements which I think it may be possible in the future definitely to prove by the ordinary logical methods of induction:

(1) In primitive societies any things that have important effects on the social life necessarily become the objects of ritual observances (negative or positive), the function of such ritual being to express, and so to fix and per-

petuate, the recognition of the social value of the objects to which it refers.

(2) Consequently, in a society which depends entirely or in some large measure for its subsistence on hunting and collecting, the various species of animals and plants, and more particularly those used for food, become the object of ritual observances.

(3) In differentiated societies of certain types (as, for example, tribes divided into sibs or clans, *i.e.*, into groups of kindred) the different segments tend to be differentiated from one another by differences of ritual, observances of the same general type for the whole tribe being directed to some special object or class of objects for each one of its segments.

(4) Consequently, while in undifferentiated societies (such as the Andaman Islanders) the ritual relation to the animals and plants used for food is a general undifferentiated relation between the society as a whole and the world of nature as a whole, in differentiated societies the general tendency is to develop special ritual relations between each of the social segments (clans or other groups) and some one or more species of animal or plant, or occasionally some special division of nature in which a number of species are included.

I cannot, of course, on this occasion, develop and explain this theory of totemism. The first and the third propositions are statements of general laws the discussion of which would involve the whole theory of ritual in general.[4] I only give you this bald statement of the theory in order to show you that it is possible to have a theory of totemism which, if substantiated, will help us to understand not only totemism but also many other things, without committing oneself to any hypothesis as to the historical origin or ori-

[4] I have already published, in a work on the Andaman Islanders, a part of the evidence for the first two statements.

gins of totemism. Further, I would point out, and insist on the point, that a theory of this kind (whether it be the one outlined above or another) is capable of verification by the ordinary processes of induction. It is true that the process of verification is a lengthy one. I first became interested in totemism some sixteen years ago, and made up my mind to begin by studying a primitive people who had no totemism, if such could be found. I found such a people in the Andaman Islands, and after working amongst them I ventured to formulate a working hypothesis on totemism in very much the form in which I have just stated it to you. I then went to Australia, where some of the most interesting forms of totemism are to be found, intending to spend there the eight or ten years that I thought would be necessary to verify this hypothesis. My work was unfortunately interrupted after little more than two years by the war, and having an opportunity I went later to Polynesia, where there are to be found what seem to be the remains of a totemic system now incorporated in a system of polytheism. So that while I cannot say that I have been able fully to verify the hypothesis, I have been able to test it by applying it over a fairly wide field. In any case I am bringing it forward here as an example not of a verified hypothesis, but of one that by its nature is capable of verification in a way that theories of the origin of totemism are not.

There is an ambiguity about that word "origin," however. In the sense in which it is used by Darwin in the title of his work on the "Origin of Species," it refers to the forces or laws that have been acting in the past and are still acting to produce and perpetuate modifications in living matter. In this sense the theory that I have outlined could also be called a theory of the origin of totemism. It deals with the forces or laws which have acted in the past and are still acting to produce and perpetuate modifications in culture, and explains by reference to them the existence of totemism in some societies and its absence in others.

But the more usual meaning attached to the word origin in general usage as well as in anthropology, has been the historical one. A particular institution comes into existence at a certain moment of time in a certain society as the result of certain events. To know its origin we must know how, and, if possible, where and when it had its beginning. It is in this sense that I am speaking of origins, and what I am trying to show you is that social anthropology does not or should not specially concern itself with origins in this sense. It is true that where we have actual historical data as to the origin of a particular institution, that knowledge may be of very great value to social anthropology. But unverified and generally unverifiable hypotheses of origins are of no use whatever in our search for demonstrable laws.

The specific social forces which it is the special business of social anthropology to study are constantly present in any society and can be there observed and studied, just as the psychologist can observe the forces at work in the behaviour of the individual.

What I am trying to make clear to you is that the continual search for theories of origin has prevented the development of social anthropology along lines which would give the most valuable results. It is not only not necessary for social anthropology to concern itself with theories of historical origins, but such theories, or the concentration of attention on them, may do a great deal of harm. Moreover, theories of origin, where we have no actual historical data, must necessarily rest on assumed general laws. Many of the theories of the older anthropology rest on an assumption that changes in culture come about through the need and desire of man to understand and explain the phenomena of the world around him; that desire leads him to formulate explanations, and these being once accepted his actions are modified by them and social customs of various kinds are developed. The classical example of this hypothesis is to be found in the theory of animism of Tylor and Frazer. Primitive man desires to explain the phenomena of dreams and of death; he formulates the hypothesis that man has a soul which survives the death of the body; and having once accepted this hypothesis he develops on the basis of it an immense mass of ritual customs such as those relating to death and burial and the worship of ancestors. Now this assumption that changes in culture do commonly take place in this way, by the desire to understand, the formulation of an explanation, and the establishment of custom as the result of the belief so reached (and this seems to be the assumption underlying many other theories of origins as well as the example I have mentioned), is a general law which requires to be proved. It may apply to some of the changes that take place in our own advanced civilizations where the desire for and the search for explanations have become of great importance through the development of science. But my own view is that it is of comparatively minor importance amongst primitive peoples, and that amongst them the basis of the development of custom is the need of action, and of collective action, in certain definite circumstances affecting the society or group, and that the custom and its associated beliefs are developed to fill this need. The discussion of this, however, would take us very far, and I am only mentioning it to show that theories of origin such as the animistic theory, or Frazer's theory of totemism, necessarily involve assumptions which, if they are true, are general laws; and that, therefore, it is necessary, before we proceed to the making of theories of origin, to scrutinise our assumed general laws and demonstrate them by a sufficiently wide induction.

You will now be able to see, I hope, whither the argument has led us. The confusion that has reigned in the study of culture, which has delayed its progress, and which has of recent years caused much dissatisfaction to its students, is the result of a failure to consider sufficiently fully the methodology of the subject. The remedy is to recognize that the two different methods of explaining the facts of culture, the historical and the inductive, should be kept carefully separated in our minds, and this will be made more easy if we recognize them as belonging to different studies with different names. Ethnology then becomes the name of the attempt to reconstruct the history of culture, and must adopt a definitely and strictly historical point of view, and must work out the special methods by which it can reach conclusions with some degree of probability. This is a view which is held by the majority of the more recent American writers, and is steadily gaining ground in Germany and England. Social anthropology will then become the purely inductive study of the phenomena of culture, aiming at the discovery of general laws, and adapting to its special subject matter the ordinary logical methods of the natural sciences. The theories of origin which have occupied so large a part in the literature of the last century are then seen to form a sort of no man's land between ethnology and social anthropology. Since they are attempts to reconstruct the history of culture they belong rather to ethnology; but since they assume, and must assume, certain general laws, they are dependent upon social anthropology for the demonstration or verification of those laws. Theories of origin, in other words, must combine the results of ethnology and of social anthropology, and at some time in the future may be able to do so with profit. But for the present the need is to get some definite and generally accepted results from social anthropology and from ethnology, and this will only be done by each keeping to its own aims and to its own special methods.

Leaving aside, then, this no man's land of theories of origin, what are we to say as to the relations to one another of ethnology and social anthropology? Social anthropology as an inductive science must rely solely on facts, and on well-authenticated observations of the facts. Where ethnology propounds hypotheses that are not fully demonstrated (and at present there are very few of the hypotheses of ethnology that can be fully demonstrated), such hypotheses cannot be used by social anthropology. For to do so would be to erect hypotheses on hypotheses —a very flimsy structure. Ethnology can supply social anthropology with a few, a very few, new facts. It can do no more. For the knowledge of what changes have taken place, and in what circumstances, social anthropology must rely on history, not on conjectural history.

But, on the other hand, I am inclined to think that ethnology will never get very far without the help of social anthropology. When Adam Smith first tried to make "conjectural history" it was on the basis of "known principles" that he sought to establish his conjectures. Any hypothetical reconstruction can only be fully successful if it is based on a sound knowledge of the laws of history. But it is only social anthropology that can provide such laws. If you will study the two volumes of the "History of Melanesian Society," in which Rivers has attempted to make an ethnological analysis of the culture of Oceania and to reconstruct its history, you will see that throughout his whole argument his conclusions rest on assumptions as to what is likely to happen in certain circumstances, for instance, what is likely to happen when two peoples of different culture meet and settle in the same island. Now all such assumptions are hypothetical general statements of the kind which it is the special business of social anthropology to deal with, and which can only be proved or made probable by induction. And the main objection to the assumptions made by Rivers is that they do not seem to be based on a sufficiently wide induction and are therefore open to doubt, so that the whole edifice raised on them is consequently shaky.

Or read Sapir's attempt to lay down the principles by which we can read what he calls "time perspective" into the facts of the local distribution of culture traits. You will find once again that he assumes, and is compelled to assume, certain general principles or laws. They may be true, or they may not, but their demonstration is a matter for the inductive method and therefore for social anthropology. And if ethnology is to use such assumptions, and I do not see how it is possible for it to avoid doing so, it must depend on social anthropology for their verification.

Once, therefore, ethnology and social anthropology are recognized as separate studies, the one historical and the other inductive, the relation between them would be one of one-sided dependence. Social anthropology can do without ethnology, but it would seem that ethnology cannot do without assumptions that belong specifically to social anthropology.

Let us now pass on to consider briefly another important matter, namely the practical value of the results that may be expected from ethnology and social anthropology respectively.

Ethnology gives us a hypothetical reconstruction of the past history of civilization, some of its results being established with a fairly high degree of probability, others being little more than plausible surmise. Its practical value in human life cannot be different in kind from that of history, and cannot certainly be greater. The bare facts of history are often very interesting in themselves. It may interest us, for example, to know that Madagascar was invaded by a people from south-eastern Asia some centuries ago. But mere knowledge of the events of the past cannot by itself give us any guidance in our practical activities. For that we need, not facts, but generalisations based on the facts. Such generalisations it is not the business of history or of ethnology to give us, and historians and ethnologists are now coming to recognize that this is so. I cannot, therefore, persuade myself that the ingenious and interesting constructions of the ethnologist will ever be of much practical value to mankind. But lest you should think that in my zeal to press the claims of social anthropology I am being unfair to ethnology I will quote to you what Professor Kroeber says in reviewing Lowie's book on "Primitive Society." Professor Kroeber is one of the most determined exponents of the strictly historical method in the study of culture, and is therefore least likely to be biassed against his own science. He writes:

If now we revert from the success of the book as the logical exemplification of a method to that method itself, what can be said of the value of this method? This admission seems inevitable: that though the method is sound, and the only one that the ethnologist has found justifiable, yet to the worker in remote fields of science, and to the man of general intellectual interests, its products must appear rather sterile. There is little output that can be applied in other sciences, there is scarcely even anything that psychology, which underlies anthropology, can take hold of and utilise. There are, in short, no causal explanations. The method leads us to the realization that such and such has happened on such and such an occasion. Human nature indeed remains the same with its conservatism, inertia, and imitativeness. But the particular forms which institutions assume evidently depend on a multiplicity of variable immediate factors, and if there are common and permanent factors they either cannot be isolated or remain as vague as the three trends mentioned. In essence, then, modern ethnology says that so and so happens, and may tell why it happened thus in that particular case. It does not tell, and does not try to tell, why things happen in society as such.

This default may be inevitable. It may be nothing but the result of a sane scientific method in a historical field. But it seems important that ethnologists should recognize the situation. As long as we continue offering the world only reconstructions of specific detail, and consistently show a negativistic attitude towards broader conclusions, the world will find very little of profit in ethnology. People do want to know why. After the absorption of the first shock of interest in the fact that the Iroquois have matrilineal clans and that the Arunta have totems, they want to know why they have them when we have not. The answer of ethnology as typified by Lowie, is in substance that there are tribes fully as primitive as the Iroquois and Arunta, who are like ourselves in that they possess neither clans nor totems. But again the justifiable question obtrudes: Why do some primitive cultures develop clans and totems while others fail to? And we say that we do not know or that diffusion of an idea did or did not reach a certain area. Now it may be contended that such questionings are naive. Yet they occur and will occur. And it would seem accordingly that ethnologists owe it to their consciences to realize clearly how limited the scope of their results is, how little they satisfy the demand—be it justified or simple—for broad results, or offer formulations that will prevent the average inquirer's relapse into the comforting embrace of easy and unsound theories. Such a realization is not marked in Lowie's volume.

And finally, however firmly scientific ideals may hold us to the tools which we use, we must also recognize that the desire for the applicability of knowledge to human conduct is an inescapable one. That branch of science which renounces the hope of contributing at least something to the shaping of life is headed into a blind alley. Therefore, if we cannot present anything that the world can use, it is at least incumbent on us to let this failure burn into our consciousness.

Serious as this comparative sterility is, it is yet preferable to the point of view which recognizes the demand, but attempts to satisfy it with conclusions derived from shallow thinking under the influence of personal predilection. After all, honesty is the primary virtue, and Lowie's soberness is a long advance on Morgan's brilliant illusions. But one sometimes sighs regretfully that the honesty of the method which is so successfully exemplified here, is not stirred into quicker pulse by visions of more ultimate enterprise.

Now while ethnology with its strictly historical method can only tell us that certain things have happened, or have probably or possibly happened, social anthropology with its inductive generalisations can tell us how and why things happen, *i.e.*, according to what laws. It is, perhaps, rash to try to foretell what will be the future results of a science that is yet in its infancy, but I would suggest that our experience of the results already attained in human life from scientific discoveries in the realm of nature, render it likely that the discovery of the fundamental laws that govern the behaviour of human societies and the development of social institutions—law, morals, religion, art, language, etc.—will have great and wide-reaching results on the future of mankind. Our recently acquired knowledge of the laws of physical and chemical phenomena has already permitted us to make great advances in material civilization by the control of natural forces. The discovery of the laws of the human mind, which is the special task of psychology, seems to hold out a promise of similar great advance in such a matter as education. Shall we not be justified in looking forward to the time when an adequate knowledge of the laws of social development will, by giving us a knowledge of and a control over the social forces, both material and spiritual, enable us to attain to practical results of the very greatest importance? That, at any rate, is my faith, and should be the faith of the social anthropologist. Who of us is there at the present time who does not feel that there are many things in the civilization of to-day that would be better changed or abolished? How to attain the desired ends is what we do not know, for our knowledge of the processes of social change is very slight indeed, and is at the best purely empirical or little more. In our efforts to deal with the maladies of our civilization we are like the empiric in medicine, though even more ignorant. He makes experiments, trying one remedy after another, with no certainty as to what the result will be. We also make, or attempt to make, our experiments on the body politic, and the only difference between the revolutionary and the rest of us is that he is prepared to take heroic measures, risking all on his faith in his nostrum. Let us first recognize our own ignorance and the need of knowledge more than empirical, and let us set to work to accumulate that knowledge by patient study, in the faith that future generations will be able to apply it in the building of a civilization nearer to our heart's desire.

This forecast of the results that we may expect from the study of social anthropology in a somewhat distant future, however, will perhaps not appeal very strongly to the "practical man" who looks for more immediate results from his expenditure. Let us glance, therefore, at the more immediate practical results that may be obtained from the study. In this country we are faced with a problem of immense difficulty and great complexity. It is the need of finding some way in which two very different races, with very different forms of civilization, may live together in one society, politically, economically and morally in close contact, without the loss to the white race of those things in its civilization that are of greatest value, and without that increasing unrest and disturbance that seem to threaten us as the inevitable result of the absence of stability and unity in any society. I am aware that there are some who would deny that there is a problem, or that it is one of any great difficulty; but I believe that thinking men are more and more coming to recognize both the difficulty and the urgency of the problem, and some have come to see that we do not possess the knowledge and understanding that are required to deal with it.

Now I think this is where social anthropology can be of immense and almost immediate service. The study of the beliefs and customs of the native peoples, with the aim, not of merely reconstructing their history, but of discovering their meaning, their function, that is, the place they occupy in the mental, moral and social life, can afford great help to the missionary or the public servant who is engaged in dealing with the practical problems of the adjustment of the native civilization to the new conditions that have resulted from our occupation of the country. Let us imagine the case of a missionary or magistrate who is wondering what are likely to be the results of an attempt to abolish or discourage the custom of *uku-lobola*. He may experiment, but he then risks the chance of producing results that he has not foreseen, so that his experiment may do far more harm than good. Ethnological theories as to the probable past history of African tribes will afford him no help whatever. But social anthropology, though it cannot yet provide a complete theory of *lobola*, can tell him much that will be of great help to him, and can set him on the path of enquiry by which he can discover more. This is only one example out of many that I might have chosen. The problem of how to get rid of the belief in witchcraft is another of the same kind, in which social anthropology can supply the missionary or administrator with knowledge and understanding without which it is very unlikely that he will be able to find a satisfactory solution of his practical problems. It is not the business of the social anthropologist to attempt the solution of these practical problems, and it would be unwise, I think, for him to attempt it. The scientist must keep himself as free as possible from considerations of the practical application of his results, and particularly so in a region of problems that are the subject of heated and often prejudiced discussion. His work is to study the life and customs of the natives and find their explanation in terms of general laws. It is the missionary, the teacher, the educator, the administrator and the magistrate who must apply the knowledge thus gained to the practical problems with which we are at present faced.

I wish that I could deal at greater length with this subject and illustrate to you the way in which a little knowledge of social anthropology would have saved us from many gross blunders in our dealings with native races. But I must pass on to the final topic of my address, which is the relation of social anthropology to ethnography.

By ethnography is meant the observation and description of the phenomena of culture or civilization, particularly among undeveloped peoples. It thus provides the facts with which both ethnology and social anthropology have to deal. In the past the work of observing and recording ethnographical data has been very largely carried out by persons who had little or no training in social anthropology, and often little knowledge of ethnology. The facts thus collected from all over the globe were then studied by the anthropologist, who often enough had never had the opportunity of making ethnographical observations for himself, and he elaborated the explanations. The result of this division of labour has been very unsatisfactory on both sides. On the one side the observations made by the untrained traveller or missionary are very often unreliable and only too frequently inaccurate. It is fairly difficult to make exact observations in physics or chemistry without a systematic training in the science. But the work of making observations in ethnography is vastly more difficult than in the physical sciences. There is no other science in which observation is more difficult, or even, I think I may say, as difficult, as this; and it has in the past suffered greatly from the lack of trained observers and the reliable descriptions that they alone can give us. That disadvantage is now being gradually overcome, and there is steadily being accumulated a mass of information collected from many parts of the world by trained observers.

But on the other side the division of labour between observer and theorist has been unsatisfactory. First, the social anthropologist had to rely on descriptions, the accuracy of which he could not control; and secondly, he was unable to test his own hypotheses by further observations, a process that is an essential part of any induction.

I feel myself that this divorce of observation and hypothesis is all wrong, and that social anthropology will never make the progress that it should until they are combined as they are in other sciences. My own experience has impressed this very strongly upon me. I have read interpretations of the customs of people whom I have visited which I am sure their authors would not have offered if they had observed for themselves the people and their customs. Then I have myself worked out hypotheses to explain the customs of certain regions, and afterwards have visited those regions, and a little actual observation has served to demolish my theories in a very short time.

If social anthropology is to progress, it must follow the rules of all induction. Facts must be observed, and a hypothesis must be found which seems to explain the facts. But these are only the first two steps of the induction, and by no means the most difficult part. The next step is to return once more to the work of observation in order to verify or test the hypothesis. We may find that the working hypothesis has to be modified, or that it has to be rejected and a new one formed. And so the process goes on until we have established our hypothesis as a theory with some degree of probability.

Now this process of induction, combining observation and hypothesis, can only be carried on by the social anthropologist in the field. I feel very strongly that it is only in this way that we can do our work properly. The student, trained not only in the scientific methods of ethnographical observation that have been worked out in the last quarter of a century by the late Dr. Rivers and others, but also in the whole theory of social anthropology, must be prepared to spend some years of his life living in as intimate a contact as possible with the people or peoples whom he is to study. He must seek not only to observe, but also to explain the customs and beliefs of these people, that is, he must seek to show how each one of them is an example of some general law of human society.

It is true that this involves the danger that observation may be influenced by preconceived theories. But all observation in ethnography is so influenced by preconceptions, and the preconceptions of the trained anthropologist are enormously less harmful than those of the average traveller or untrained though educated man on whom we have had to rely in the past for information about uncivilized peoples.

Let me sum up as briefly as possible the argument that I have put before you. The systematic study of civilization was begun in the middle of the last century. At first it was not very sure of itself, of its aims and methods. Its followers were inclined to accept theories, methods, and evidence that we should now question or reject. But it was only through the work of these men that the science was able to develop. Since the end of the century determined efforts have been made to introduce stricter methods, both in observation and in interpretation. One result of this is that we have now a vastly greater body of accurate information about the culture of uncivilized peoples, and in the light of our new knowledge many of the early generalisations prove to be unsound. In the matter of methods of interpretation, the most notable tendency has been an increasing insistence on the historical point of view and the historical method of explanation, resulting in the recognition as a separate study of what I am here calling ethnology, strictly limited to the hypothetical reconstruction of the past, and excluding all generalisations, all attempts to formulate laws. In particular the older theories of evolution have been called in question, and by very many have been entirely rejected.

Meanwhile the other method of study, the inductive

method, by which we seek to make generalisations and discover natural laws of human society, has been somewhat neglected. There have been two reasons for this. One has been that the anthropologists busied themselves seeking not laws but origins. The other has been the confusion of this subject with psychology, which still exists in the minds of many students of civilization, and leads them to regard any attempt to study the customs of primitive people from the inductive point of view as being the business of the psychologist.

For the future of the study of civilization, therefore, it is necessary to distinguish these two different methods, and this will be easier if we use separate names for them and call the one ethnology and the other social anthropology. But the two, though separate, are connected. In particular, I believe that ethnology will not be able to proceed very far without the help of social anthropology; the reconstruction of the history of civilization cannot be accomplished without a knowledge of the fundamental laws of the life of societies.

Further, I have argued that from social anthropology we may expect results of far greater practical value, not only in the more or less remote future, but also in the immediate present, than we can possibly hope for from ethnology.

Thus I have been pressing the claims of social anthropology as against those of ethnology. Ethnology has received, in recent years, in England, Germany and America, more than its fair share of attention, while social anthropology, except in France, has suffered undeserved neglect. This is, I think, sufficient justification, if justification be required, for this attempt to obtain recognition of its importance and its practical value.

The present time is, I think, a critical one for the study of primitive culture. After three-quarters of a century of effort it is at last finding its feet. It is becoming clearly conscious of its aims and methods, of its own possibilities and limitations. It has, not without long struggles, been given recognition at universities and elsewhere as a science amongst other sciences. It is now in a position, I believe, to give results that may be of immense practical value, more particularly to those who are concerned with the government or the betterment of backward peoples. In recent years there have been an increasing number of students trained in strict methods of observation and with the knowledge of the subject that is required for research in the field. Meanwhile, just as the science is, as it were, coming of age, its subject matter is disappearing with great rapidity. The spread of the white race and of European civilization over the world has produced in a century or two immense changes. Native peoples in many regions have been extinguished, as the Tasmanians, or are approaching extinction, as the Australians and our own Bushmen. Elsewhere, though the people survive, their customs and their mode of life are changed. They no longer make the things they formerly made, they learn a new language, their customs fall into disuse, and many of their former beliefs become forgotten. The very material on which the ethnologist and the social anthropologist rely for their studies is disappearing before our eyes. There is, I think, no other science that is in this position. There is no other in which work which is not done at once will never again be possible.

For this reason, then, the urgency of work that cannot wait, and also because of its great importance in relation to the practical problems with which this country is faced by reason of the native population which surrounds us, I would suggest that there is no more valuable way in which this Association could at the present time carry out its aim of the advancement of science than by encouraging and assisting in every way possible the science of social anthropology and the scientific study of the native peoples of this continent.

References

GRAEBNER. Methode der Ethnologie. Heidelberg, 1911.

RIVERS. The Ethnological Analysis of Culture; Presidential Address to the Anthropological Section of the British Association for the Advancement of Science, 1911.

RIVERS. The History of Melanesian Society; 2 vols., 1914.

KROEBER (A. L.). Eighteen Professions. *American Anthropologist*, Vol. 17, page 283. 1915.

HAEBERLIN (H. K.). Anti-Professions. A Reply to Dr. A. L. Kroeber. *Ibid.*, page 756.

SAPIR (E.). Time Perspective in Aboriginal American Culture. A Study in Method. Ottawa, 1916.

SWANTON (JOHN R.). Some Anthropological Misconceptions. *American Anthropologist*, Vol. 19, page 459. 1917.

BOAS (FRANZ). The Methods of Ethnology. *American Anthropologist*, Vol. 22, page 311. 1920.

SCHMIDT. Die kulturhistorische Methode und die nordamerikanische Ethnologie. *Anthropos*, Band XIV–XV, page 546. 1920.

Chapter II

HISTORICAL AND FUNCTIONAL IN-TERPRETATIONS OF CULTURE IN RELATION TO THE PRACTICAL APPLICATION OF ANTHRO-POLOGY TO THE CONTROL OF NATIVE PEOPLES [1]

Anthropology is gradually establishing its claim to be regarded as a study which has an immediate practical value in connection with the administration and education of backward peoples. The recognition of this claim is responsible for much of the recent development of anthropological studies in the British Empire—the appointment of government anthropologists in Ashanti, Nigeria, Papua and the Mandated Territory of New Guinea; the provision of training in anthropology for officers entering the colonial services in Africa; the establishment of the School of African Life and Language in Cape Town in 1920 and the more recent establishment of a school of anthropology at Sydney. This development has raised the question "What sort of anthropological investigations are of practical value in connection with such problems of administration?" The work of the ethnographer who merely collects information about native life and custom is of course of value. But a science does not confine itself to collecting data; it must also interpret them. When we come to deal

[1] Abstract of a paper read before the fourth Panpacific Science Congress at Java, 1929.

with the facts of culture there are two methods of inter-pretation, which may be called the historical and the func-tional. When we adopt the historical method we "ex-plain" a culture, or some element of a culture, by showing how it has come to be what it is as the result of a process of historical development. The method is applicable at its best only when there are full historical documentary rec-ords. For uncivilized peoples where we have no such records the application of the historical method consists of making hypothetical reconstructions of the past. A very great deal of anthropological theorizing during the last half-century has taken this form. The weaknesses of this method are (1) that the hypothetical reconstructions remain hypothetical, being incapable of verification: (2) that their validity depends on that of the assumptions (generally implicit) on which they are based, assumptions as to the nature of culture and the laws of its develop-ment: (3) that, consequently, it does not really explain anything at all—history only *explains* when it shows us *in detail* the relation between a culture as it is at a given moment and actual conditions and events in a known past. In relation to our present discussion the greatest weakness of the method of interpreting culture by hypo-thetical reconstructions of the unknown past is that it is entirely devoid of any *practical* value. At the best we can only claim for it an academic interest. The functional method of interpretation rests on the assumption that a culture is an integrated system. In the life of a given com-munity each element of the culture plays a specific part, has a specific function. The discovery of those functions is the task of a science that might be called "social physiol-ogy." The postulate on which the method depends is that there are certain general "physiological" laws, or laws of function, that are true for all human societies, for all cul-tures. The functional method aims at discovering these general laws and thereby at explaining any particular element of any culture by reference to the discovered laws. Thus, if it is a valid generalisation to say that the chief function of ritual or ceremonial is to express and thereby maintain in existence sentiments that are necessary for the social cohesion, we can "explain" any given ritual or ceremonial by showing what are the sentiments expressed in it and how these sentiments are related to the cohesion of the society. History, in the narrow sense does not and cannot give us general laws. The hypothetical reconstruction of the past inevitably assumes certain general principles but does not prove them; on the contrary its results depend on their validity. The functional method aims at the discovery and verification of general laws by the same logical methods as those in use in the natural sciences—physics, chemistry, physiology. When knowledge is to be put to practical use it must be generalised knowledge. To exercise control over any group of phenomena we must know the laws relating to them. It is only when we understand a culture as a functioning system that we can foresee what will be the results of any influence, intentional or unintentional, that we may exert upon it. If, therefore, anthropological science is to give any important help in relation to practical problems of government and education it must abandon speculative attempts to conjecture the unknown past and must devote itself to the functional study of culture.

Chapter III

THE PRESENT POSITION
OF ANTHROPOLOGICAL
STUDIES[1]

In this address which I have the honour to make to you as
the president of this section, I shall lay before you certain
considerations as to the present position of anthropological studies. It might perhaps be regarded as my duty to
make a survey of the history of these studies and what has
been accomplished in them during the hundred years over
which we are now, as an Association, looking back. But
this address had to be written during a journey from one
side of the world to the other, so that it was not possible
for me to have access to the necessary books. Moreover,
as between looking back over the past and looking forward to the future, I have a temperamental preference for
the latter.

Anthropology, as that term is currently used, as for example in defining a university curriculum, is not one subject, but includes several somewhat related subjects while
excluding others not less related. If we define anthropology as the science of man and of human life in all its aspects, then it is obvious that psychology, as the study of
the human mind or human behaviour, must be included
in anthropology between human biology, which deals
with man's physical organism, and social or cultural anthropology, which deals with his social life. Yet actually

[1] Presidential address to Section H of the British Association for
the Advancement of Science, Centenary Meeting in London, 1931.

not only is psychology not commonly included in what is called anthropology, but there is very little systematic co-ordination between psychological and other anthropological studies. The reason for this lies in the history of psychology, which was first developed in close relation with, or indeed as part of, philosophy. It is only gradually that psychology has been differentiated from philosophical studies, and by adopting precise methods similar to the experimental methods of the natural sciences has established itself as an independent scientific discipline. It seems to me that the time is now ripe for psychology to sever its connection with the philosophical subjects of logic and metaphysics and bring itself into closer relation with anthropology. This is not merely a question of a logical arrangement of the sciences. Both psychology and the other anthropological sciences will benefit greatly by a more systematic co-ordination.

Leaving aside psychology, then, we now find the general field of what is called anthropology divided into three separate portions. One of these may best be named Human Biology, for the term Physical Anthropology is commonly applied in a somewhat narrower sense to cover only part of that field. In one part of this field, in Human Palaeontology, we have witnessed in the last fifty years many important discoveries, of which the latest, Dr. Davidson Black's determination of *Sinanthropus pekinensis*, is certainly one of the most significant. In another part of Human Biology, the study of comparative racial anatomy, which is what is usually understood by the term Physical Anthropology, a great amount of work has been done in the way of measurements on the living subject and in the study of skeletal material. I cannot help feeling myself that the results obtained have not been by any means proportionate to the time and energy expended. I believe that one of the reasons has been the preoccupation with attempts to reconstruct the racial history of mankind, when we have as yet no precise knowledge of how varieties of the human species actually come into existence. I think we ought to look forward in the field of Human Biology to a closer co-operation of comparative racial anatomy with Human Genetics, and also to a further development of comparative racial physiology, in which so far much less work has been done than in anatomy.

The natural and most useful association for Human Biology is with the other biological sciences, with general biology, the results of which it has to apply to, or verify in, the human species, with comparative morphology and physiology, and with palaeontology. There is much less benefit to this subject in a close association with prehistoric archaeology or with social anthropology.

Human Biology (or Physical Anthropology) and Social Anthropology meet together in connection with two sets of problems. One of these is the effect of social institutions on the physical characters of a population. This study seems to me to fall within the sphere of Human Biology rather than in that of Social Anthropology, for it requires to be handled by one who is by training a biologist. The other problem is the reverse of this, namely, the discovery of what differences, if any, in culture are the result of racial differences, *i.e.* of inherited physical differences of different peoples. Now this problem, or this set of problems, can only be approached by means of a study of comparative racial psychology, or the comparative psychology of peoples. For it is obvious that any inherited physical differences between races will act chiefly through psychical differences in any effect they may have upon culture. Thus, the recent researches of Prof. Shellshear bid fair to enable us to define certain morphological differences of the brain as differentiating the Australian aborigines from the Chinese, and the latter in turn from Europeans. The determination of what mental differences are correlated with these differences of cerebral structure is a task for the psychologist or psycho-physiologist.

Comparative racial psychology, which is thus closely connected with Human Biology, is a subject of great difficulty in which little progress has been made as yet. The first task is that of providing a technique for determining with as much precision as possible the average psychological differences between different populations. Many of these differences are very obviously the result of differences of culture, and the ultimate task of such a study, of proving that certain observable psychological differences are correlated with differences in the physical organism, and are therefore strictly racial differences, is one that we cannot yet hope to approach as a scientific problem.

Another field that lies within the general field of Anthropology as now organised is that of Prehistoric Archaeology. I need not remind you how greatly this subject has developed and prospered in recent years. It has won far more popular interest and support than any other branch of Anthropology. At the same time it has become more definitely a specialised study. It has thus attained an independence that it did not possess when anthropological studies were first organised in associations and universities.

Besides these two subjects, Physical Anthropology, or, as I think it might be better called, Human Biology, and Prehistoric Archaeology, Anthropology as now organised includes as a third field the study of the languages and cultures of non-European peoples, and particularly of those peoples who have no written history. This separation of the peoples of the world into two groups, one of which is studied by the anthropologist, while the other is left to historians, philologists and others, is obviously not justifiable by any logical co-ordination of studies, and is no longer so fully justified by practical considerations as it was when it first arose. Changes that are taking place in this field will soon require, I think, a different organisation of our studies in relation to others.

It is to this branch of anthropology, the study of the cultures of non-European peoples, that I wish to devote my attention in this address. Of the changes that have recently been taking place in it, which are important and significant for its future development, there is one which I will here only mention and will return to it later. In its earlier development the study was a purely academic one, having no immediate bearing on any particular aspect of practical life. This has now changed, and there is a growing recognition that the study of the life and customs of a tribe of Africa or New Guinea by an ethnographer or social anthropologist can be of practical assistance to those engaged in governing or educating that tribe. Anthropology, or this branch of it, is now being brought into close relation with colonial administration, and we may anticipate many important results from this association.

This new position of anthropology will, I believe, help to hasten forward the development of a change of point of view in the study, a change of orientation, which has been slowly making itself felt during the last few decades, and with which I propose to deal at some length. I will attempt to state in a few words what this change of orientation is. Using the word science to mean the accumulation of exact knowledge, we may distinguish two kinds of scientific study, or two kinds of method. One of these is the historical. The other method or type of study I should like to call the inductive, but there is a chance that the word might be misunderstood. I will therefore call it the method of generalisation. This distinction between the historical and the generalising sciences was emphasised long ago by Cournot. It is one of great importance in any question of scientific methodology.

Now when the study of non-European peoples was first undertaken, it was very natural, and indeed inevitable, that it should be treated by the method of the historical sciences so far as those methods were applicable. But during the past hundred years there has been a steadily growing movement towards the creation of a generalising science of culture or society. The moment has come when the existence and independence of this science should be recognised.

I have said that in the early stages of the study of non-European peoples the approach made was that of the historical point of view. One of the tasks of history is to give us accurate descriptions of a society or people at a given time. The ethnographer's work of describing to us a non-European people was taken up precisely in this way. But history also gives us chronological accounts of the changes in a people's life. For the European peoples we have written documents that enable the historian to do this. For many non-European peoples we have no such records. The ethnologist, true to the assumption that history was what he wanted, engaged in the attempt to supply a conjectural or hypothetical history.

The procedure began in the eighteenth century, when attempts were made to identify native peoples in different parts of the world as the descendants of the ten lost tribes of Israel, or similarities of custom with ancient Egypt were interpreted as the result of Egyptian influence. The identification of the lost ten tribes of Israel seems to be no longer the concern of anthropologists, but the ingenious tracing of the most diverse customs all over the world to a hypothetical origin in Egypt still survives, and, as it seems to possess a strong emotional appeal for certain minds, will probably persist.

Towards the end of the eighteenth century, with Adam Smith and others in England and France, the hypothetical reconstruction of the past took another form. It was supposed that in some sense the less developed peoples represented early stages in the development of our own culture.

The aid of knowledge about them was therefore called in to help in creating a conjectural history which dealt with such general matters as the origins of language or of civil government, and so on.

Thus from early times the attempts to utilise information about non-European peoples took two distinct forms. It will be convenient to have different names by which to distinguish the two studies, and I shall use the word ethnology to refer to one and shall speak of the other as belonging to social anthropology. This conforms fairly well to the ordinary usage of these two terms.

Ethnology, in the sense in which I am here using the word, is concerned with the relations of peoples. If we study the existing peoples of the world, and those of the past about which we have information, we are able to define certain similarities and differences in racial characters, in culture and in language. The ethnologist may confine himself to determining as precisely as possible these similarities and differences and so providing a classification of peoples on the basis of race, language and culture. If he seeks to go further and explain them he does so by hypothetical historical processes. It is evident that throughout the period of human life on the planet there have been movements and intermingling of races; there has been spread of languages, and the subsequent differentiation of one language into several distinct languages; and there have been movements of whole cultures with the migration of peoples from one region to another, or spread of particular elements of culture through the interaction of neighbouring peoples. The present situation of the peoples of the world, or the situation at any moment of history, is the result of the total series of changes that have taken place over some hundreds of thousands of years. The aim of the ethnologist is to make hypothetical reconstructions of some of these processes.

Ethnology, as thus defined, is a historical and not a

generalising science. It is true that in making their historical reconstructions the ethnologists often assume certain
generalisations, but as a rule little or no attempt is made
to base them on any wide inductive study. The generalisations are the postulates with which the subject starts, not
the conclusions which it aims to attain as the result of the
investigations undertaken.

Social anthropology, in the sense I am giving to that
term, has concerned itself with a different type of problem. It has interested itself in the development of institutions in human society. From its earliest beginnings it attempted a sort of compromise between the two different
scientific methods, the historical and the generalising.
Undoubtedly one of the aims of Social Anthropology has
been to understand the nature of human institutions and,
if I may use the phrase, how they work. But instead of
adopting outright the methods of the generalising sciences, social anthropology was dominated by the conception of history, of historical explanation and the historical
method. And since historical records were insufficient it
endeavoured to make a hypothetical history of institutions and of the development of human society. It discussed such matters as the origin of language and of religion, the development of marriage and of property, the
origins of totemism and exogamy, or the origin and development of sacrifice or of animistic beliefs.

Social anthropology frequently sought the origins of
social institutions in purely psychological factors, *i.e.* it
sought to conjecture the motives in individual minds that
would lead them to invent or accept particular customs
and beliefs. Its explanations were frequently, or even
usually, historical in one sense, but psychological in another, almost never sociological. This point will be returned to later.

Throughout almost the whole of the last century this
historical-psychological method so dominated anthro-

pological study that it was hardly possible for any one to escape from it. Thus, when Robertson Smith laid the foundations of the scientific study of religions and took up the problem of the nature of sacrifice, (for that, as we should now see it, was really the problem,) he was not content to isolate and classify the different varieties of sacrifice, and show their relation as different forms of a widespread type of religious rite—that would be the method of the modern sociologist, as represented in the essay of Hubert and Mauss—but the strong tradition of his time made him attempt to fit the different varieties of sacrifice into a scheme of historical development whereby one variety was supposed to have had its origin in another.

The compromise that social anthropology made between the historical and the generalising methods was one impossible to maintain. As a result there have been in the last few decades two movements, one towards ethnology and the other towards sociology, and the traditional social anthropology has been subjected to criticism of different kinds from these two quarters.

Throughout almost the whole of the nineteenth century there was little distinction between ethnology and social anthropology. Tylor, for example, combined the two studies. It is true that some writers followed by preference one study to the exclusion of the other. Thus Sir James Frazer has rarely concerned himself with ethnological problems. It is also true that the two methods occasionally came into conflict over particular problems, but this conflict did not become one between the two methods and the two points of view.

Towards the end of the last century and in the earlier part of this century there developed, in America, in Germany and in England, schools of ethnologists which, while disagreeing amongst themselves on particular questions of historical reconstruction, and even on the methods of ethnological analysis, yet all joined in attacking the methods of social anthropology from the point of view of historical method. These criticisms of what the ethnologists call "evolutionary anthropology" are familiar to all of you.

The shift over from social anthropology to ethnology is illustrated in the development of the ideas of the late Dr. Rivers. I think I can speak with some knowledge of Rivers, for I was for three years his pupil in psychology, and was his first pupil in social anthropology in the year 1904. Rivers was from first to last primarily a psychologist, and was an inspiring teacher in psychology. He had no training in ethnology or in archaeology, and only gradually made a partial acquaintance with those subjects. In his first period of interest in anthropology, from the time of the Cambridge Expedition to Torres Straits to the year 1909, his conception of the aims and methods to be followed in the study of non-European peoples was that of what I have been describing as social anthropology. Even if he could not regard Morgan's theories, for example, as being satisfactory, he yet assumed that the making of theories of that type was the task of the anthropologist, and I believe that even up to the end of his life he still accepted in general outline the animistic theory of Tylor and Frazer. Ultimately, during his work in Melanesia, his growing dissatisfaction with that method came to a head, and in 1911, in his presidential address to this section, he declared his allegiance to the ethnological method. In other words, from one type of historical study he transferred his attention to another. In the years 1913 and 1914 I had much discussion with Dr. Rivers on the subject of anthropological method by correspondence and in personal interviews, partly because at that time he did me the kindness to read and criticise, in manuscript and in proof, a book that I was writing. His view at the time our discussions ceased was that, while he was fully prepared to grant the validity and the necessity of the method of comparative sociology, he regarded the method of ethnology as equally valid and necessary and at the same time independent, and that he preferred to devote his own attention to the latter rather than the former. At the very end of his life there were indications that his attitude was changing once more, that he was growing somewhat dissatisfied with the ethnological method which he so stoutly defended in 1911, and that he was directing his attention to the method which I am here speaking of as that of Comparative Sociology.

In the change of point of view that he made in 1911 Rivers was therefore representative of a general tendency. There had been a growing dissatisfaction with the theories of social anthropology. From the point of view of a desire for historical explanation that dissatisfaction is, I think, justified. A historical study "explains" by revealing particular relations between particular phenomena or events. History does not generalise or cannot legitimately do so. It shows us that at a given moment a particular event occurred, and as a result of this something else happened. Thus, a cause in historical explanation is something which happened once and was followed by certain results. It is not similar to what is called a cause in natural science, which is an event that recurs or may recur repeatedly and always produces the same effect. Historical explanation is always concerned with particulars, normally with showing a chronological relation between two or more particulars. The value of historical explanation is therefore directly proportional to the amount of certain and detailed knowledge that we have of the events with which we are concerned.

It may be said in one sense that the ethnologist *explains* the existing similarities and differences between peoples by means of his historical hypothesis. Actually, however, he is not interested, at any rate primarily, in explanation. Where he attempts a reconstruction of history it is because he wishes to discover something about a past of which we have no records in written documents. He is interested in a knowledge about the past, as far as it is attainable, for its own sake. Or if the ethnologist believes himself to be following some other aim, then he is pursuing the wrong method. All that his hypothesis can give him will be a certain number of more or less probable statements about the past. And his results will only be valuable or valid if he avoids basing them on assumptions as to general principles of historical change which have not been demonstrated by sociology, for it is the specific task of sociology to discover such principles.

The methodological difficulty in ethnology is, and always will be, the demonstration of its hypotheses. I do not suppose that anyone has ever accepted, or ever will accept, Rivers's elaborate reconstruction of the history of Melanesia. The theories of culture cycles, that are held so firmly by some ethnologists that they speak of them as though they were demonstrated beyond any possibility of doubt, are totally rejected by other competent and open-minded students. The Egyptian theory of the origin of culture has its special devotees, but so has the Atlantis theory.

It is certain that the ethnological method carefully used may give us a very limited number of highly probable, if not quite certain, conclusions. Thus there is no doubt that the language of Madagascar and a good deal of its culture are derived either from Indonesia or from some region from which the Indonesian languages and culture were also derived. In such an instance we are dealing with a great number of resemblances between the two regions which cannot be otherwise explained, and the matter of the languages is conclusive. Similarly it might be possible to demonstrate some sort of general relationship between Australia and South India, or between Indonesia and

Melanesia. But it seems to me highly doubtful if we can ever obtain from ethnology any considerable mass of proven detailed knowledge of the historical relations of peoples and regions.

I believe that this feeling is shared by many anthropologists whose interest still attaches to history. In the last thirty years or so we have watched the development of several diverse schools of ethnology or culture-history. Some of these have offered us elaborate schemes of reconstruction of the whole of human history; others have dealt with particular local problems. But it is impossible to reconcile the different theories with one another or even to discover principles of method about which there is general agreement. To say nothing of theories of the derivation of culture from a lost Atlantis or a lost Pacific continent, we are offered a choice between the Egyptian theory championed in its latest form by Prof. Elliot Smith, or the theory of culture-cycles of Graebner, or the somewhat different theory of Father Schmidt, or that of Frobenius, and I know not how many more. Each school goes its own way building up its own hypothetical structure, not attempting to seek out points on which agreement can be reached with others. The procedure is often that of disciples of a cult rather than that of students of a science. The result is that many would-be ethnologists, seeing how much hypothesis and how little certainty there is in these reconstructions of history, have been turning to archaeology, in which at least some certainty and general agreement can be reached. This movement I think is a thoroughly sound one. Where written documents are absent it is first of all to archaeology that we must look to give us some knowledge of the history of peoples and cultures.

If then we set out to study human life by the methods of historical science, we aim at discovering everything that we can of interest about the past. When written records are available we make use of them, and such study is called history in the narrow sense. We may supplement the written records by investigations in archaeology. This study has reached a stage when it can give us precise and certain information within a limited field. It can only tell us about those things in the life of a people that can be directly inferred from their material remains. Ethnology can to a limited extent supplement history and archaeology.

The historical interest in human life is one of the chief motives for the study of non-European peoples. But the same study offers scope for another interest, the desire to reach a scientific understanding of the nature of culture and of social life. In the past those two interests have been often confused. The progress of our studies requires that they be separated, and this separation has been taking place during the last few decades. Out of social anthropology there has grown a study which I am going to speak of as Comparative Sociology.

By this term I wish to denote a science that applies the generalising method of the natural sciences to the phenomena of the social life of man and to everything that we include under the term culture or civilisation.

The method may be defined as being one by which we demonstrate that a particular phenomenon or event is an example of a general law. In the study of any group of phenomena we aim at discovering laws which are universal within that group. When those laws are discovered they "explain" the phenomena to which they refer. A science of this kind, as I conceive it, still remains descriptive, but in place of descriptions of particulars and their particular relations, such as the historical sciences give us, it provides general descriptions.

The older social anthropology did not follow this method, at any rate consistently. We have seen that it devoted most of its attention to formulating hypotheses about the origins of social institutions. Nevertheless social anthropology, by its comparative study of institutions, made possible the development of comparative sociology. I could, if I had time, show you how the new anthropology, *i.e.* comparative sociology, grew gradually out of the older study; how the first tentative movements towards this science began in the eighteenth century; how the work of such men as Steinmetz, Westermarck and others, and particularly that of Emile Durkheim and his followers, led step by step to the present position in which we can claim that there is now in existence a comparative sociology which demands recognition as something radically different in important respects from the social anthropology out of which it has grown.

The essential difference between the older social anthropology and the new lies in the kind of theories that one and the other seek to establish by the study of the facts. As I see it, comparative sociology rejects, and must reject, all attempts at conjecturing the origin of an institution when we have no information based on reliable historical records about that origin.

I can only hope to make my meaning in this matter clear to you if you will permit me to refer to a particular example. We may take as our example totemism, which has received a good deal of attention in social anthropology. Totemism is a name which we apply to a large number of different kinds of institutions in different cultures, all having in common the one feature that they involve some special relation between social groups and natural species, usually species of animals or plants. It is to be noted, first of all, that totemism is not a simple concrete thing; it is an abstraction, a name applied to a number of distinct and diverse things which have something in common. What is or is not included under the term depends on the definition we adopt, and different writers choose different definitions.

The older social anthropology concerned itself with the question of the origin of totemism. Even supposing that we have settled what we are and what we are not to include under the term, our question is still not specific. If we try to make it specific we must recognise that there are three possibilities. One is that all the things we call totemism in Asia, Africa, America and Oceania are historically derived from some one particular institution which had its origin in a particular region at a particular time. A second is that some one particular form of totemism may have arisen independently in two or more regions at different times as the result of similar historical processes, and that existing varieties of totemism are all derived from this. The third is that different forms of totemism may have had their origin independently in different regions at different times by different historical processes. If I had to decide which of these three possibilities seemed to me the most likely, I should select the third. And this would mean, of course, that totemism has not had *an* origin.

In many of the theories of totemism it is difficult to tell whether the author is thinking of the first or the second of the two possibilities mentioned above. Prof. Elliot Smith, however, definitely adopts the first. If I understand him he would regard everything all over the world that he calls totemism (and I am not sure what he would include in or exclude from that term) has been derived in comparatively recent times from Egypt, where the particular institution from which they are so derived had its origin a few thousand years ago, an origin determined by the particular form taken by Egyptian civilisation.

Sir James Frazer's final theory of totemism is well known to you. It assumes that all existing forms of totemism are derived from one simple original form. In making an assumption of this kind Prof. Elliot Smith and Sir James Frazer agree, but their agreement goes no further. The particular form selected by Sir James Frazer is what he calls conceptional totemism, the belief that the foetus in a mother's womb is derived from some food (animal or vegetable) that the mother has eaten. The belief is known to exist in parts of Australia and Melanesia, and I should think that, if it were sought for, it might quite well be found in other regions from which it has not been recorded. This, then, on Sir James Frazer's theory, gives us the historical origin of totemism. It is not clear whether he conceives this form of totemism to have come into existence only once at a particular time in a particular spot, or whether he conceives it as having come into existence in different regions at different times. In completion of this theory he offers us a psychological explanation of the belief which, for him, is the germ out of which all diverse forms of totemism developed. Man, not being aware of the physiological causes of impregnation, but being desirous of finding some explanation, was led to the conception that food eaten by a woman and followed by sickness (the sickness of pregnancy) was the cause of the pregnancy, with which it was thus associated.

I do not intend to offer you criticisms of these two theories of totemism. If criticism is to consist, as I think it always should in science, of a re-examination of the evidence adduced in favour of a hypothesis, I cannot see that any evidence has yet been offered for the historical reality of either of these hypothetical processes. Indeed, I find it impossible to imagine what real evidence of that kind could be discovered.

For comparative sociology, totemism presents a different problem or series of problems. These may be described as being concerned with the nature and function of totemism. To elucidate the nature of totemism we have to show that it is a special form of a phenomenon much more widespread, and we must aim at demonstrating that it is a special instance of a phenomenon or at any rate of a tendency which is universal in human society. For this purpose we have to compare totemism with all other possibly related institutions in all cultures.

From the outset of our inquiry, therefore, we cannot isolate totemism and deal with it as a separate thing. First of all totemism in any given culture is part of a more extensive system of beliefs and customs, and may occupy a preponderant position in that system, as in many Australian tribes, or may occupy a small and almost insignificant position. In different cultures totemism is not the same thing.

When we examine totemism by the sociological method, the first thing we discover is that it is merely a special example, or rather a collection of special examples, of a larger class, namely of ritual relations established by the society between human beings and objects of nature such as animals or plants, and such things as rain. We find that there are important systems of beliefs and customs establishing such ritual relations which are not included under the term totemism. We find them among people such as the Eskimo or the Andaman Islanders, who have no totemism. The problem of totemism thus becomes a part or aspect of a much wider problem, that of the nature and function of the ritual relations between man and animals and plants in general. Thus, many years ago I wrote what was intended to be a direct contribution to the sociological theory of totemism in the form of a study of the relations between man and natural species in a non-totemic people, the Andaman Islanders.

This problem, however, which is wider than the problem of totemism, is itself merely a small part of a still wider problem, that of the nature and function of ritual and mythology in general. If we wish to know why certain peoples treat wild animals and plants as sacred things, we must discover the general principles on the basis of which things of all kinds are treated as sacred. Thus the problem of totemism, as soon as it is fully stated, leads straight to one of the fundamental problems of Sociology, that of the nature and function of ritual and myth. This is characteristic of the sociological method, that any problem, however small, is part of a general fundamental problem of the nature of culture and of human society.

Nevertheless we must, and we can, partially isolate particular problems for special study. The provisional conclusions we reach will be subject to revision when the particular problem we are dealing with is considered in relation to the general problem of which it is part.

Without attempting the impossible task of trying to fit in to a brief statement the theory of the nature of ritual in general, I think we can formulate one important principle which is relevant to the problem of totemism. This is that in societies in which the whole population, or the major portion of it, is engaged in immediate subsistence activities, those things which are of vital importance in relation to subsistence become important objects of ritual. Perhaps we may be more cautious and say that there is a strongly marked tendency for this to happen. For there are possible exceptions, such as the lack of any record of a cattle cult amongst the Hottentots.

Special examples of this law or tendency are the cattle cults of pastoral peoples, the corn cults of tillage people, and the weather and season cults of peoples of all kinds. The treatment of wild animals and plants as objects of ritual by hunting and collecting people is partly or very largely to be regarded as simply another special example of this general tendency. Other factors come in, with which I have not time to deal, but once we recognise their possibility they need not affect our argument.

We have thus reached one provisional generalisation covering those customs and beliefs of which totemism is a part. But the special character of what is commonly regarded as the normal form of totemism is that the whole society is divided into segments (moieties or clans), and there is a special ritual relation between each segment and some one or more species. This can also, I think, be shown to be a special example of a general law or tendency whereby in any segmentary structure, which has a religious basis or function, the solidarity of each segment, the differentiation or opposition between the segments, and the wider solidarity which unites the segments into a larger whole in spite of that opposition, are expressed and maintained by establishing a ritual relation between the whole society and certain *sacra* and by establishing a special relation between each segment and some one or more of these *sacra*. Totemism of clans or moieties is only one example of what is a much more widespread general phenomenon in the general relation of ritual to social structure.

There would, of course, be very much more than this in a general sociological theory of totemism. There are a great many different kinds of totemism, and their relations to one another and to the theory would all have to be considered. But the general method would be the same, seeking, in relation to each particular phenomenon we examine, to see it as a particular example of a widespread class.

By pursuing this process of analysis and generalisation we can come to see totemism as a particular form taken by what seems to be a universal element in culture. Every culture that we know has some system of beliefs and customs by which the world of external nature is brought into a relation with society in which the two form a single conceptual structure, and relations are established between man and nature of a kind similar in certain respects to the relations established within the society between the human beings themselves. I am inclined to regard it as one of the essential functions of religion to provide this structure. Our own relations to a personal God who has created or who is regarded as maintaining the natural order, is an example of what I mean. The fully developed or elaborated totemism of a people like the Australian aborigines is an example of the same general or universal process. It establishes a whole system of special social solidarities between men and animals, plants, and other phenomena of nature.

When we have in some such way as this arrived at a satisfactory conception of the nature of totemism we can proceed to a study of its functions. By the function of an institution I mean the part it plays in the total system of social integration of which it is a part. By using that phrase, social integration, I am assuming that the function of culture as a whole is to unite individual human beings into more or less stable social structures, *i.e.* stable systems of groups determining and regulating the relation of those individuals to one another, and providing such external adaptation to the physical environment, and such internal adaptation between the component individuals or groups, as to make possible an ordered social life. That assumption I believe to be a sort of primary postulate of any objective and scientific study of culture or of human society.

When we take up the functional study of totemism, then we must examine in each particular case of a sufficient number, what part the special variety of totemism of a given region plays in the total system of integration which the whole culture provides. We might study in this way the functions of a number of different varieties of totemism in Australia, and then draw certain general conclusions as to the function of totemism in the general integrative system of Australian tribes. We should not thereby be entitled without examination to draw conclusions as to the functions of totemism in America, or India, or Melanesia, or Africa.

Just as the question of the nature of totemism is part of a very much wider sociological problem, so the study of the functions of totemism is part of the general sociological problem of the function of religion.

The foregoing brief and inadequate statement of how I conceive that comparative sociology will take up the problems of totemism will, I hope, have served the purpose for which it was introduced, namely, to illustrate the difference of method that distinguishes the newer social anthropology from the old. I have chosen the subject of totemism because some of the most important steps of the passage from the old to the new methods are to be seen in Durkheim's treatment of this subject in his "Elementary Forms of the Religious Life." Unfortunately, Durkheim retained some of the ideas and some of the terminology of the older social anthropology. He speaks of his study as aiming to determine the "origin" of totemism, and although he seeks to give a new meaning to the word "origin," yet his use of it misleads most of his readers, and I think it really misled Durkheim himself and caused him to cast what is really a theory of the nature and function of totemism into a form which renders it open to criticism, and which has caused it to be misunderstood by many of his readers.

I think we should use the term origin, in speaking of any institution, as meaning the historical process by which it came into existence. Thus we can speak of and actually study the origin of Parliamentary Government in England. In comparative sociology, if we are to make it the science it should be, we must reject absolutely all attempts to conjecture the origin of any institution or element of culture. Wherever we have good and sufficient documentary evidence as to the origin of anything this can of course be utilised by sociology, but that is an entirely different matter.

I have pointed out that the theories of the older social anthropology often took a psychological form. The procedure was one of conjecturing processes of thought in the minds of individuals which would lead them to adopt a certain belief or custom. I have not time in this address to discuss the subject of the relation of sociology to psychology. There is still a great deal of confusion as to that relation. The position maintained by the sociologist is (1) that in social institutions and in the phenomena of culture generally the sociologist has a field of study which is entirely distinct from that of the psychologist, and that generalisations made in this field must be sociological and not psychological generalisations; (2) that therefore any explanation of a particular sociological phenomenon in terms of psychology, *i.e.* of processes of individual mental activity, is invalid; (3) that ultimately the nature of human social life is determined by the nature of the psychophysical organism of man, and that therefore when we have discovered universal sociological laws it will be the duty of the psycho-physiologist to discover their basis in psycho-physical processes; (4) that, on the other hand, the behavior or the psychology of an individial human being is largely determined by the culture which has been imposed upon him by the society in which he lives.

The sociologist therefore claims that it is possible and necessary to distinguish psychology and sociology as two distinct subjects, just as distinct as physics and chemistry. It is only when the two subjects are so distinguished that it will be possible to obtain real co-operation and co-ordination between them.

The newer social anthropology then, as I see it, differs from the older in several vital respects. It rejects as being no part of its task the hypothetical reconstruction of the unknown past. It therefore avoids all discussion of hypotheses as to historical origins. It rejects all attempts to provide psychological explanations of particular social or cultural phenomena in favour of an ultimate psychological explanation of general sociological laws when these have been demonstrated by purely sociological inquiries. It endeavours to give precise descriptions of social and cultural phenomena in sociological terms, and to this end seeks to establish a suitable exact terminology, and seeks at the same time to attain to a systematic classification of those phenomena. It looks at any culture as an integrated system and studies the functions of social institutions, customs and beliefs of all kinds as parts of such a system. It applies to human life in society the generalising method of the natural sciences, seeking to formulate the general laws that underlie it, and to explain any given phenomenon in any culture as a special example of a general or universal principle. The newer anthropology is therefore functional, generalising and sociological.

Although the newer anthropology rejects much of the methods of the older, and rejects all the theories of origins with the elaboration of which the latter was so much concerned, yet the new anthropology has grown out of the old, would not be possible without it, and starts with valuable knowledge of social phenomena and some insight into their nature which were incidentally provided by the earlier anthropologists in their search for origins. The work of such men as Tylor, Robertson Smith, Frazer, Westermarck, to mention only some of the greatest and of this country only, paved the way for the advance that we are now making. In rejecting the conclusions they reached by what we regard as an unsound method, we do not forget all that we owe to them in the first systematic exploration of the regions we now seek to survey more exactly and with new instruments.

Comparative sociology, as I am here calling the newer form of anthropology, requires a new conception of the aims and methods of field investigations amongst non-

European peoples. It is not so very long ago since for most of our information about the life and customs of such peoples we had to rely on the writings of persons who had no training for the work of observation and description, travellers and missionaries principally. It is now recognised that we can no more rely on such information than we could rely on the observations of an untrained person in such a science as geology. The first point, therefore, in relation to field research is that to have its full value for scientific purposes the description of the culture of a non-European people must be based on the careful work of a thoroughly trained observer.

During the last forty years there has been a considerable quantity of work carried out in this way, particularly in America. Under the influence of Dr. Haddon in England and Prof. Boas in America, a good deal has been done in developing a technique of ethnographical fieldwork.

It is true that we still meet with persons who regard themselves as competent to carry out such work of observation without the preliminary training. One also still finds writers who quote from accounts of missionaries and travellers, as if their records were as reliable as those of trained specialists.

As ethnographical field-work has become in recent years more systematic, observation has tended to become more extended and more penetrating. Earlier ethnographical descriptions were mostly confined to the more accessible aspects of a culture, its formalised elements. The result was normally a very incomplete picture of the life of a people. Recent work, such as that of Prof. Malinowski or Dr. Margaret Mead, gives us, as the result of more extended and methodical observation, valuable information about what may be called the unformalised aspects of the life of a people such as the Samoans, the Trobriand Islanders, and the Admiralty Islanders. Without informa-

tion of this kind we can never hope to make full comparative use of any description of a culture.

Comparative sociology involves another and perhaps
even more important change in the conception of the nature of field research. On the older view the task of the
field-worker was simply to observe the facts and record
them as precisely as possible with the help of such concrete material as photographs, texts in the native language, and so on. It was not his business, at any rate as a
field-worker, to attempt any interpretation of the data he
collected. This he could leave to others who would make
it their business.

The conception of the newer anthropology is the opposite of this, and is that only the field-worker, the one
actually in contact with the people, can discover the
meaning of the various elements of the culture, and that
it is necessary for him to do this if he is to provide material to be fully utilised for the purposes of science.

When I speak of the "meaning" of an element of culture, I use the word very much as we do when we speak of
the meanings of words. If we consider an individual, the
meaning of a word that he hears or uses is the set of associations that it has with other things in his mind, and
therefore the place it occupies in his total thinking, his
mental life as a whole. If we take a community at a given
time the meaning of a word in the language they use is
constituted by the associations normally clustering around
the word within that community. Therefore the maker of
dictionaries collects examples of the usage of a word and
tries to classify and, as far as possible define, the different
varieties of usage.

Now the meaning of an element of culture is to be
found in its interrelation with other elements and in the
place it occupies in the whole life of the people, *i.e.* not
merely in their visible activities, but also in their thought
and feeling. The discovery of this with any certainty is

obviously only possible for one who is living in actual contact with the people whose culture is being studied, and as the result of systematic directed investigation. It is true that when we have a somewhat full knowledge of a people and of all aspects of their culture, we can form ideas as to the meaning of their customs and beliefs. Thus I think that it is possible in the case of the Eskimo to be fairly certain that the essential meaning of the Sedna myth lies in its relation to the division of the year into two parts, summer and winter, and the effects this division has on the social life. But even so, the full elaboration of this hypothesis, and still more the actual verification of it, the demonstration that this really is the meaning, could hardly be carried out except by further investigation amongst the natives themselves.

It must not be supposed that the meaning of an element of culture can be discovered by asking the people themselves what it means. People do not think about the meanings of things in their own culture, they take them for granted. Unless we are anthropologists we do not think about the meaning of even such familiar customs amongst ourselves as shaking hands or raising the hat. If by chance the ethnographer comes upon an individual who has thought about the meaning of his people's customs, he is likely to give what is his own individual interpretation which, significant and interesting though it may be, cannot be taken as a valid statement of what the custom really means to the community in general. The meaning of any element of culture can only be defined when the culture is seen as a whole of interrelated parts, and this can only be accomplished by one who is able to take an objective view of it, the ethnographer or descriptive sociologist, in fact.

The field-worker, therefore, has to follow a special technique for discovering the meanings of the facts of culture that he observes, a technique analogous in some ways to, but on the whole more difficult than, that used by the lexicographer in recording a spoken language for the first time. This technique is now being slowly developed, but its full development will only be possible as progress is made in sociological theory.

From the point of view of the comparative sociologist much of the work done in the recording of the cultures of non-European peoples in the past is unsatisfactory and cannot be properly utilised. The cases of our ethnographical museums are filled with objects the full meanings of which we do not know and probably can never discover. Our libraries are full of collections of myths obtained from native peoples, and books containing detailed and illustrated accounts of ceremonies, without anything to reveal to us the meanings of those myths or ceremonies. Such material can, of course, be put to some use by the sociologist, but it is of decidedly less use than it is to be hoped that field-work of the modern type will be.

I think that the first movement towards this new kind of field-work was made many years ago by Dr. Haddon when he organised the Cambridge Expedition to Torres Straits. In those days, however, it was thought that the proper person to undertake the systematic interpretation of a culture would be a psychologist. Dr. Haddon took with him three of the foremost psychologists of our times. The experiment had valuable results, but that general interpretation of the Torres Straits culture, that was to have been included in the volume of the Reports dealing with Psychology, will never be written. The psychologist as such is not qualified to undertake the task of interpreting culture. It is a task that belongs not to psychology but to sociology. Dr. Haddon's conception came too soon in the history of anthropology.

As France led the way in the development of the theoretical study of comparative sociology, we might have expected that it would be in France that the new methods of field-work would be elaborated. The work of Doutté in Morocco was an early step in that direction, and the later work of Réné Maunier is a good example of the new methods. Marcel Granet's important work on China is based rather on the study of Chinese documents than on observation of the living culture. But the French apparently are not drawn very strongly towards ethnographical research.

At the present time it is only in the work of a small but increasing number of investigators that the new methods are illustrated. I can indicate the work of Prof. Malinowski and of Dr. Margaret Mead. But during the next few years we may expect to see the publication of a good deal of work carried out on these lines.

An objection that is and can be raised against this kind of work is that there is a great deal of room for the personal equation of the investigator to influence the results. That is true and must be recognised, but its importance can easily be exaggerated. A remedy, not perhaps perfect but very valuable, will lie in the development of a technique or methodology of interpretation, whereby the validity of a particular interpretation can perhaps be demonstrated by crucial facts or at any rate tested in such a way as to reduce, if not eliminate, the effects of the personal equation. The elaboration of this technique is one of the problems that faces us at the present time, one of the urgent needs of our science. The multiplication of studies of this kind, by bringing a larger number of observers into the field, and by providing us in some instances with observations in one region by two independent workers, and also the occasional co-operation of two or more persons in one investigation, will all help towards the elimination of the effects of the personal equation. But the most important thing of all in this direction will be the development of sociological theory which will afford a guide to the field-worker in his studies and assist him to obtain both objectivity and completeness in his observations.

An adequate sociological understanding or interpretation of any culture can only be attained by relating the characteristics of that culture to known sociological laws. These laws can of course only be discovered by the comparative method, *i.e.* by the study and comparison of many diverse types of culture. The procedure in our science must therefore depend on the building up of a body of theories or hypotheses relating to all aspects of culture or social life and the testing of these hypotheses by intensive field research. The field-worker of the future, or indeed of the present, must be thoroughly cognisant of all the sociological hypotheses that are partly verified, and if possible of those in course of elaboration, and must direct his research to the testing of these hypotheses, either his own or those of other workers in the science, by their application to a particular culture. Only in this way can the hypotheses be tested and either verified, rejected, or modified; and the normal result will probably be modification rather than complete verification or complete rejection. Only so can the proper method of the generalising sciences be carried out, namely, the process of making a preliminary study of the known facts, the formulation of hypothetical generalisations, the testing of these hypotheses by a further examination of a specific series of data, the modification of the original hypotheses in the light of the new data, the further testing of the hypotheses in their new and possibly more complex or more definite form, and so on. Only in some such way as this, in default of the possibility of actual experiment, can we build up a science of human society.

I have said that the meaning of any element of a culture is to be found by discovering its relation to other elements and to the culture as a whole. It follows from this that the field-worker must normally, or whenever possible, undertake an integral study of the whole culture. It is not possible, for example, to understand the economic life of a native people without reference to such things as the system of magic and religion, and of course the converse is equally true. The necessity for such unitary intensive studies of selected areas was long ago insisted on by Dr. Haddon and later by Dr. Rivers, and may be said to be part of the tradition of the Cambridge school. The development of the sociological point of view has made the necessity even more evident than before.

It may be noted here that this view of the unitary nature of culture is one of the most important features of the new anthropology, and a point in which it differs markedly from some of the former and present-day anthropology and ethnology. Certain writers on culture adopt what might perhaps be called an atomic view of culture. For them any culture consists of a number of separate discrete elements or "traits" that have no functional relationship with one another, but have been brought together as a mere collection by a series of historical accidents. A new element of culture has its origin somewhere and then spreads by a process of "diffusion," which is frequently conceived in an almost mechanical way. This point of view has arisen largely from the museum study of culture.

The new anthropology regards any persisting culture as an integrated unity or system, in which each element has a definite function in relation to the whole. Occasionally the unity of a culture may be seriously disturbed by the impact of some very different culture, and so may perhaps even be destroyed and replaced. Such disorganised cultures are very common at the present day all over the world, from America or the South Seas to China and India. But the more usual process of interaction of cultures is one whereby a people accepts from its neighbours certain elements of culture while refusing others, the acceptance or refusal being determined by the nature of the culture itself as a system. The elements adopted or "borrowed" from neighbours are normally worked over and modified in the process of fitting them into the existing culture system.

The scope of field-work amongst non-European peoples is being widened in another direction, partly as a result of the new conception of the theoretical aims of the study, and partly as a result of the relations now being established between anthropology and colonial administration. In former days if a field-worker went to a people who had been subjected to European influence, as was usually the case, his task was to discover as far as he could, and in detail, what the original culture was, before that influence took effect. It was not considered a part of the ethnographer's work to study in detail the changes produced in the native culture by the contact with Europeans. But a precise knowledge of these changes and how they occur is often of great value for theoretical sociology, and even more for the provision of a scientific basis of exact knowledge for colonial administration. The ethnographer's first task remains the same, that of learning all that it is possible to discover about the culture as it was originally. Only after that has been done with some measure of completeness is it possible to understand the changes that European influence brings about. But if anthropology is to be of real assistance to colonial administration the field-worker must now undertake to study and interpret the changes which he finds taking place in the culture he is investigating.

Such studies are, however, of little or no value either for sociological theory or for practical purposes when the culture in question is in process of complete disintegration or destruction, as, for instance, amongst the Australian aborigines or some of the tribes of North American Indians.

In the new anthropology, therefore, the work of field research has become much more difficult and of much wider scope. The selection and training of persons for that work is also more difficult. The field-worker should be equipped with a thorough knowledge of all the latest developments of theoretical sociology. At the present time this cannot be obtained from books, but only by personal contact with those who are working in the subject. Then he should have learnt the technique of field-work, both as to observation and interpretation. Further he must have a knowledge of all that has been so far learnt about the culture of the culture region in which he is to work, and if possible some knowledge of the languages also. Finally the success of a field-worker in ethnography often depends on certain qualities of temperament and character. Not everyone can win the confidence of a native people.

It is obvious that the ideal field-worker is not easy to find, and needs some years of training. Yet the rewards of the career are much less even than those of other sciences. One of the great difficulties in this science is that of finding workers and providing the means for them to carry out their work. Research in social anthropology is generally expensive. It cannot be carried out, as so much scientific work can, within the precincts of a university. A most urgent need is the provision for such research by means of research fellowships which would enable the anthropologist who has been trained for field-work to carry out such work over a span of years without having to abandon it in favour of a teaching or other appointment, such as at present is the only way of attaining an assured and continuous income.

Yet the future of the comparative sociology of non-European peoples lies entirely with the field-worker. The

day has gone by when we could accept the scientific authority, in this study, of any one who has never himself
made an intensive study of at least one culture. In the past
we have owed a good deal to those who have been called
"armchair anthropologists." But in the present situation
of the science no insight, however genial, can fully com-
pensate for the absence of direct personal contact with the
kind of material that the anthropologist has to study and
explain.

This, then, is still another important feature of the new
anthropology, the insistence that research and theory
must not be separated but must be as closely united as
they are in other sciences. The observations of the data,
the formulation of hypotheses and the testing of these
hypotheses by further direct observation are all parts of
one single process which should be carried out as far as
possible by the same individual.

Meanwhile there is one fact that seems to me at times
to make the position of our science almost tragic. Now
that by the gradual development of theory and the improvement of methods of investigation we are in a position to make the most important contributions to the science of man by the intensive and exact study of the less
developed cultures of the world, those cultures are being
destroyed with appalling rapidity. This process of destruction, through the combined action of European trade or
economic exploitation, government by European officials,
and missionary activity, is taking place with accelerated
pace. During the twenty-five years since I first took up
this work myself I have seen great changes. Tribes in Australia and Melanesia and in North America from which
we could have obtained most valuable information a
quarter of a century ago will now afford us little, or in
many instances nothing. In another quarter of a century
the position will be ever so much worse. Work that is still

possible in all parts of the globe will then be forever impossible. Is there any other science, or has there ever been another science, faced with such a situation, that, just at the time it is reaching maturity, but while through lack of general interest and support it has few workers and very scanty funds, a great mass of most important material is vanishing year by year without the possibility of making any study of more than a minute fraction.

It will be through field researches that anthropology makes progress towards becoming a real and important science. But intensive studies of single cultures or societies are not sufficient in themselves. Such intensive studies must themselves be inspired and guided by theory, and theoretical sociology must rest on the comparison of different cultures one with another, for comparison in this science has very largely to take the place of experiment in other sciences.

The newer anthropology is developing a different conception of the comparative method from one that has been current in the past. In the older anthropology we were offered books or monographs in which similar, often only superficially similar, customs or beliefs were collected from all sorts of cultures all over the world and thrown together. It was this that was in fact often thought of as constituting the comparative method. Such a procedure may be useful in giving a first survey of some particular problem or group of problems, and has been useful in that way in the past. But it can never do more than indicate problems, it cannot solve them. For that, a more precise and more laborious procedure is necessary.

To understand what precisely the comparative method should be we must bear in mind the kind of problems to the solution of which it is directed. These are of two kinds, which we can distinguish as synchronic and diachronic, respectively. In a synchronic study we are concerned only with a culture as it is at any given moment of its history. The ultimate aim may be said to be to define as precisely as possible the conditions to which any culture must conform if it is to exist at all. We are concerned with the nature of culture and of social life, with the discovery of what is universal beneath the multitudinous differences that our data present. Hence we need to compare as many and as diverse types of culture as we possibly can. In the diachronic study of culture, on the other hand, we are concerned with the ways in which cultures change, and seek to discover the general laws of such processes of change.

It seems to me evident that we cannot successfully embark on the study of how culture changes until we have made at least some progress in determining what culture really is and how it works. Thus the study of synchronic problems must necessarily to some extent precede the study of diachronic problems. The changes that take place in the institutions of a people are not properly comprehensible until we know the functions of those institutions. On the other hand, it is also true that if we can study changes taking place in some aspect of culture it will help us greatly in our functional investigations.

As the problems of comparative sociology are of two kinds, so the comparative method will be used in two ways. In relation to the synchronic study of culture we shall compare one with another different cultures as each exists at a given moment of its history, and without reference to changes in the culture itself.

The loose comparative method, as it was often used, and indeed is still used by some writers, is scientifically unsound in that it makes immediate comparisons between isolated customs or beliefs from different regions and from cultures of very different types. Further, it concentrates attention on similarities of custom, and often on what are only apparent and not real similarities. But for the sociologist the differences are certainly not less important than the resemblances in culture, and the new comparative method concentrates its attention on these differences.

I have already indicated how comparative sociology regards a culture as normally a systematic or integrated unity in which every element has a distinct function. It therefore aims, and must aim, at comparing whole culture systems one with another, rather than comparing isolated elements of culture from diverse regions. The procedure, therefore, has to be analogous to that of the comparative morphologist and physiologist in the comparison of animal species. They carry on their studies by comparing varieties within the same species, or species within the same genus, and then proceeding to the comparison of genera, of families and of orders.

In comparative sociology, as Steinmetz pointed out many years ago, scientific procedure must be based on a systematic classification of cultures or of social types. Our first step, therefore, is to define as well as we can certain culture areas or types of culture. The procedure, of course, is as old as Bastian, but has acquired a new importance and use.

Thus we find that Australia as a whole is a single sufficiently homogeneous area, having the same type of culture throughout. We can therefore immediately proceed to a comparison of the various Australian tribes one with another. Each tribe, or each small group of tribes, can thus be regarded as offering us in its culture system a special variety of a general type. By studying these variations as minutely as possible we can carry out a process of generalisation which enables us to give a general definition or description of the type itself. By this process we are often able to discover correlations between one element of culture and another. Further, this procedure is almost essential in any attempt to discover the meaning and the function of any element. For by it we are able to determine, in any institution or custom or belief, what remains constant and what varies as between one part of a culture area and another.

This study of culture types and varieties in comparative sociology is quite different from the study of culture-areas in ethnology. The latter aims, above all, at providing material for the hypothetical reconstruction of movements of culture diffusion. The former is essentially a process of generalisation, a means of discovering general features or principles which remain constant throughout the type while taking different forms in different parts of the area.

In this study of variations of a single culture type we should aim at comparing the whole culture of one tribe with that of another. But that is often impossible; in fact, in the present state of our knowledge, almost always. We may proceed, therefore, by making a comparative study of variations in some particular aspect of the culture. But we must be careful how we isolate one part of the culture from another for the purposes of study. Thus, a good deal of misunderstanding has resulted from dealing with some particular aspect of the social organisation of Australian tribes, instead of dealing with that organisation as a whole.

There is perhaps no other region which is quite the same as Australia in the opportunities it offers for the study of many variations of a single culture type. In other regions, therefore, our procedure must be somewhat different. Thus if we wish to deal with the Bantu cultures of Africa we must begin by dividing the whole region into suitable units. One such unit would be composed of the Basuto-Bechuana tribes, while the Zulu-Kaffir tribes would provide us with another. Our first step will consist of a careful study of the variations within the unit region. We then compare the one region with the other, and may proceed in this way to explore the whole Bantu area in such a way as to be able to give a sound description of the general characters of Bantu culture as a whole. Only when we have carried studies of this kind a certain distance does it become really profitable to make comparisons between Bantu culture and Polynesian or North American.

Thus, for the new anthropology the comparative method is a method of obtaining generalisations. Amongst the variations of institution and custom in one region we seek to discover what is general to the whole region or type. By comparing a sufficient number of diverse types we discover uniformities that are still more general, and thus may reach to the discovery of principles or laws that are universal in human society.

A word, the constant use of which has been a great obstacle to scientific thinking in anthropology, is the word "primitive." It conveys the suggestion that any society to which we apply it represents for us something of the very beginnings of social life. Yet if culture had, as we may well assume, a single origin some hundreds of thousands of years ago, then any existing culture has just as long a history as any other. And although the rate of change may vary, every culture, just as every language, is constantly undergoing change. But, quite apart from this implication of the word as meaning in some sense "early," harm is done by the current application of it to the most diverse types of culture. The difference of culture between the Maori of New Zealand and the aborigines of Australia is at least as great as that between ourselves and the Maori. Yet we group these two cultures together as "primitive," and contrast them with our own as "not primitive." I am well aware how difficult it is to avoid completely the use of the term, or some equally unsuitable one, such as "savage." Perhaps if we keep sufficiently in mind the great cultural differences between the various peoples whom we thus lump together we shall avoid the chief disadvantage attaching to its use. We shall then be able to avoid the fault of the loose comparative method, of regarding as immediately comparable with one another all those very different types of society that are labelled primitive.

This abstract discussion of method, I fear, will hardly convey to you any very definite conception. Will you permit me, therefore, to select a particular example of a synchronic problem and indicate briefly the lines along which I would attempt to solve it? We may take for our example one of the fundamental problems of sociology, that of the nature and function of the moral obligations which a society imposes on its members. For the purposes of scientific investigation this general problem must be subdivided into a large number of subsidiary problems. Thus we can isolate, as one such, the problem of the nature and function of the rules prohibiting marriage between persons who stand in certain social relationships; in other words, the nature and function of the prohibition of incest. These prohibitions were, of course, dealt with by the older social anthropology, and we have had a number of theories of the "origin" of the prohibition of incest. Even Durkheim faced this problem in the old way. Now, quite apart from the fact that any hypotheses as to how prohibitions of this kind first came into existence many hundreds of thousands of years ago are entirely incapable of verification, it is also evident that even a plausible hypothesis of origin can give us no explanation of the great diversity that we find in the prohibitions current in different existing social types. Yet it is the explanation of these differences that is really the crux of the problem. In this, as in so many other sociological inquiries, we have to seek an explanation *per genus et differentiam.* We wish to know why every society has rules of this kind and why the particular rules vary as they do from one social type to another. As soon as we state the problem in this way, we have a comparative problem of the kind I have been referring to. In dealing with such a problem I would first select a culture in which the rules prohibiting marriage are definite and highly elaborated. The culture of the Australian tribes is obviously in this respect a very suitable one. Further, we must have a culture in which there are sufficient variations between one tribe and another, while the general type remains the same. Here again Australia is a very suitable region. I would therefore begin the investigation by a comparative study of Australian tribes. Note that this is not at all because Australian culture is "primitive" in the sense that it represents the early beginnings of human society. On the contrary, Australian culture is a highly specialised one, in which there has been an extreme elaboration of the kinship organisation, and it is exactly for this reason that I would select it for the study of any problems relating to kinship. Australia represents not the beginning but the end of a long line of development of kinship structure. Thus, my reasons for selecting Australia are the exact opposite of those put forward by earlier writers who have made the same selection.

Having selected a first field for comparative study I would compare the social organisation, as a whole, of all the Australian tribes about which we have adequate information, in order to define what is the nature of the correlation between the rules prohibiting marriage and the social structure. In other words I should be seeking to define as precisely as possible the function of such rules as part of the total system of social integration. The investigation has to rest on the detailed examination of variations. As the result of such a study of Australia we can reach a number of significant generalisations. We shall, for example, reach certain provisional conclusions as to the nature (not the origin) of exogamy. These conclusions must now be tested by a similar study of other types of culture. It would be impossible for one student even in a lifetime to make a thorough investigation of all known cultures in this way. That is why the co-operation of a number of students in the study of any single problem is so essential in sociology. But a close study of one other type of culture sufficiently different from the Australian would permit of a very valuable verification of the provisional results obtained.

When a theory as to the nature and function of the prohibition of incest has thus been reached, the next step will be to seek for the *experimentum crucis* by which it can be more critically tested. Such a crucial instance will often be one which appears to conflict directly with the theory. Thus, on my own theory we ought to find marriage everywhere prohibited between parent and child and between brother and sister. The various societies in which the marriage of brother and sister is permitted, therefore, offer us an opportunity of testing the theory, for we must be able to explain these exceptions on the basis of the theory itself. The exception must prove the rule. Other similar crucial instances can be sought by which to test the validity of the general theory.

As a result of such an investigation we should, if we are at all successful, reach certain conclusions as to the relation between moral obligations and social structure. In other words, we should have learnt something about the place of such obligations in social integration. Sociology would then have to undertake similar investigations on other problems within the general problem. We might study in the same way the obligations relating to the taking of human life, or those relating to the rights of property. As the final result of such a series of related studies we could arrive at a theory of the nature and function of morality in general. Incidentally, of course, any single investigation of this kind must be linked with and throw light on a great number of other sociological problems. Thus, the study of the prohibition of incest necessarily involves a close study of kinship from other aspects also.

I hope that the example I have given will have made it clear that the comparative method as used for the synchronic study of culture is something different in important respects from the older comparative method used as a means of arriving at theories of the origin of institutions.

When we turn to the diachronic problems with which comparative sociology has to deal, *i.e.* with the problems of how cultures change, the comparison of cultures as each of them is at a given moment of history, while it may give us a certain amount of help, is not sufficient by itself. Thus, the study of the variations that have been produced in a single culture, as, for example, in Australia, although we have no observations as to how or when they occurred, can nevertheless give us our preliminary orientation in the study of how variations do occur. In other words, the comparative study of cultures without history is a method of enabling us to formulate with some precision the problems with which we shall have to concern ourselves in a diachronic study of culture.

Ultimately, however, if we are to discover the laws of social change we must study the actual processes of change. This we can do to some extent by means of historical records, wherever we have records that are sufficiently reliable and complete. But it is desirable that as soon as possible the sociologists themselves should undertake to study the changes that take place in a culture over a period of years. The comparative method in this instance will consist in the careful comparison of accurately observed processes of change.

In the present organisation of anthropology the social anthropologist is supposed to confine himself to the study of the peoples without history, the so-called primitive or savage peoples who still survive outside Europe. If he considers Europe at all he is supposed to concern himself only with prehistoric times and with what is called folk-lore, *i.e.* certain aspects of culture which have been regarded as survivals from earlier, more primitive, cultures. This division of the peoples of the world into two groups for the purpose of study was apparently satisfactory enough, as long as anthropology was dominated by the historical method. The historian could give us the real history of European languages and cultures throughout historic times. It was left to the anthropologist, as ethnologist or archaeologist, to concern himself with the reconstruction of the past in those regions and periods that lay outside the field of history proper.

But for comparative sociology as the generalising science of culture, this division of the historic and the non-historic cultures is entirely unsuitable, and indeed detrimental. The sociologist must study all cultures and by the same methods. In dealing with historical cultures he is not competing or conflicting with the historian, for the two follow quite different aims and methods. The historian does not or should not seek generalisations. He is concerned with particulars and their particular and generally chronological relations.

I am sorry that I have not time in this address to deal properly with the relation of the study I have described as comparative sociology, and the studies pursued sometimes under the name of sociology or social science. I can do no more than offer a few brief remarks. First let me say that what is called sociology in France, or at any rate at the University of Paris, is the same study precisely as that which I have been desribing as comparative sociology, and it is largely owing to the work of the French sociologists Durkheim, Hubert, Mauss, Simiand, Halbwachs, Hertz, Granet and Maunier, to mention only some of them, that the subject is as far advanced as it is.

In Germany a great deal of what is called sociology is really better described, I think, as social philosophy or philosophy of history. One writer who represents the comparative sociology that I have described is Richard Thurnwald.

In England we have very little of anything that is called sociology. Hobhouse, who stood for sociology in this country, was a philosopher rather than a scientist.

In the United States there are a great number of departments of sociology scattered through the universities. It is difficult to summarise the various kinds of study that are included under the term. A considerable part of the work in many departments of sociology consists of what would be called civics in this country and in studies connected with social welfare work. There is still a little of what should properly be called social philosophy, though much less than there was a quarter of a century ago. The most marked activity of these departments at the present time is what can be described as factual social studies, *i.e.* the collection of precise information, in statistical form wherever possible, about certain aspects of social life, principally in the United States itself, but also to some extent in other countries.

I think I have made it clear that my own view is that any attempt to discover the general laws of human society must be based on the thorough detailed study and comparison of widely different types of culture. It was, indeed, the very firm conviction that this was so that led me to enter the field of anthropology a quarter of a century ago. I am, if anything, more convinced than ever of this, and see no hope for the development of any really scientific sociology except on this comparative basis.

Unfortunately, what has happened has been that anthropology has largely neglected the sociological study of non-European peoples in favour of conjectural history, and at the same time most of those engaged in one form or another of sociological study have had little thorough knowledge of non-European societies. What I have described as comparative sociology has, except in France, been left by the anthropologists to sociology, and by the sociologists to anthropology. I believe that the unsatisfactory results of this division of studies, whereby comparative sociology has failed to find any proper place, is now coming to be recognised in America, partly as the result of the work of the Social Science Research Council in attempting to co-ordinate the various social studies, and I live in hope that before another quarter of a century is out the science of comparative sociology will have obtained a recognised and very important place in any well-organised school of social sciences.

English universities, or I may say British universities in general, have been very chary of admitting sociology in any form as a subject of study, in strong contrast with the popularity of the subject in the United States. To some extent that caution has been a wise one. The subject is still in its formative stages. But, on the other hand, its absence from the list of recognised university studies has stood very much in the way of its development.

You will see that in this address I have been chiefly concerned with trying to indicate a new alignment of the studies which are grouped together under the name Anthropology. This new alignment is itself a natural growth, but should be recognised, and must ultimately be made the basis of any satisfactory co-ordination of studies in universities and elsewhere.

First, there are the three studies that have traditionally associated under the name anthropology—Physical Anthropology, Prehistoric Archaeology and Ethnology.

Physical Anthropology seems due to be absorbed in a wider study of Human Biology, which requires to be carried on in close association with the biological sciences. The present procedure by which Physical Anthropology is taught as part of Anatomy is not always quite satisfactory. It is liable to neglect the physiological study of man as a living organism, and to deal very perfunctorily with the important problems of human genetics. I should like to see Human Biology given recognition as an independent and very important subject. We have, of course, the Galton Laboratories as one centre for such studies in England. The widespread interest—not always, I fear, entirely scientific—in Eugenics and in race problems could be utilised to obtain sufficient support. On the other hand, there seems no particular advantage to Human Biology in being linked to Archaeology and Ethnology.

Prehistoric Archaeology is now an independent subject with its own special technique and carried on by specialists. The archaeologist, of course, requires to have a knowledge of Human Palaeontology, but equally he needs a knowledge of general palaeontology and geology. The natural affinity of Archaeology, however, is with History.

Ethnology, in so far as it attempts not merely to classify races, languages and cultures, but to reconstruct their history, must necessarily maintain a very close connection with archaeology. It may, indeed, very well be treated as in a sense a branch or further development of archaeology, as that is of history. Thus, Prehistoric Archaeology (or Palaeo-ethnology as it is occasionally called) and Ethnology may well be regarded as one subject pursuing the aims and methods of historical science.

Over against the historical sciences there stand the three generalising sciences of Human Biology, Psychology and Comparative Sociology.

The closest and most important relation for Comparative Sociology is with Psychology. There is no particular advantage to the comparative sociologist in acquiring more than an elementary knowledge of Prehistoric Archaeology. A study of history, so far as it deals with culture rather than with the doings of kings, statesmen and soldiers, is of much greater value to him. Particularly at the present time it is desirable that the comparative sociologist should avoid becoming entangled in the conjectural reconstructions of history which I have described above as belonging to Ethnology.

As I see it, therefore, the subject of anthropology is dividing itself into three subjects, distinguished either by differences of method or of subject-matter; Human Biology, which is, or should be, allied with the biological sciences; Prehistoric Archaeology and Ethnology, which belong with historical studies; and Comparative Sociology, the relations of which are with psychology on the one side and on the other with history and with the social sciences, economics, jurisprudence, etc.

I have said nothing yet on the study of languages. We have witnessed in recent decades the development of a general science of Linguistics which has been winning for itself an independent place. It is, I think, highly desirable that a close connection should be maintained between Linguistics and Comparative Sociology. I have no time on this occasion to discuss in detail the relations of the two subjects.

In concluding this address I wish to return to a matter that was briefly mentioned at the beginning, namely, the very important recent development of what we may call Applied Anthropology or Administrative Anthropology. During more than a decade my own work has been very largely concerned with this study in Africa and in Oceania. If I seem to you to speak dogmatically in what I have to say, I would ask you to remember that in the time at my disposal I can only put before you certain of my conclusions without explaining the considerations on which they are based.

For a very long time the anthropologists have been declaring the necessity of utilising their science in the practical work of governing and educating dependent peoples. So far as the British Empire is concerned this has at last led to certain practical steps being taken. There have been appointments of Government anthropologists in two of the African colonies, and in Papua and the Mandated Territory of New Guinea. Cadets and officers of the services of the African colonies are now given brief courses of instruction in anthropology at Oxford and Cambridge. In South Africa the School of African Life and Languages of the University of Cape Town started some years ago a vacation course on anthropology and native administration and education for government officers and missionaries, and I believe that these courses have been continued. In Sydney a more extensive experiment has been carried on since 1927. Cadets who are selected for the administration of the Mandated Territory are sent to the territory for one or two years to make acquaintance with the kind of life and work they will have, to test their suitability for it and to enable them to judge if they do finally wish to take up the career. They then attend the University of Sydney for one academic year of nine months and devote their whole time there to a special course of training. This includes two short courses in Topographical Surveying and in Tropical Hygiene, but the greater part of their time is devoted to the study of Comparative Sociology and Colonial Administration. The result of this arrangement will be that in a certain number of years all the administrative officers of the territory will have a sound knowledge of the principles and methods of Comparative Sociology, and by its means will have acquired a considerable knowledge of New Guinea institutions and customs and their meaning, and will have made a systematic study of administrative problems and methods. The cadet system has not been accepted by the territory of Papua, but a number of the senior officers of the administration have devoted their vacations to attending special courses at Sydney.

Thus, some progress has already been made in turning anthropological studies to practical use. There is still a great deal more that might be done and that ought to be done. Some of the British colonies, such as the Western Pacific and British Malaya, have neither government anthropologists nor any regular training in anthropology for their officers. Moreover, it seems to me that the courses now taken by officers in the African services are inadequate. A few weeks given to anthropology may be better than nothing, but certainly cannot be called sufficient. There is no doubt that one of the most efficient native administrations is that of the Dutch East Indies, and the qualification for this requires five years of special studies, including native languages and native law and custom.

A question of some importance is, what kind of anthropological teaching should be given to native administrators to fit them better for carrying on their work. There is, I think, no value to them in a study of physical anthropology or the classification of races that falls under physical anthropology or ethnology. There is equally no value for them in any study of prehistoric archaeology. Further, those attempts to reconstruct the history of cultures and peoples that I have been calling ethnology are of absolutely no practical value in the work of native administration or education.

There is obvious practical value in training which will help the colonial officer to speak the language or languages of the peoples he is dealing with. This is already well provided for in some of our colonies.

What the administrator and educator amongst dependent peoples need above all is a detailed knowledge of the social organisation, the customs and beliefs of the natives and an understanding of their meanings and their functions. This can be attained only by means of a general study of comparative sociology, followed by an intensive study of the particular people in question.

I have on many occasions met with persons who were engaged in the government or education of native peoples who have expressed the view that, whatever academic interest anthropology might have, it has no practical value in work such as they are engaged in. I have found that what was thought of as anthropology by these persons was the series of academic studies that includes physical anthropology, the classification of races, the ethnological reconstruction of history, prehistoric archaeology and the social anthropology that elaborates theories of the origins of institutions. One magistrate complained to me that, though he had read the whole of the *Golden Bough*, he did not find that it gave him any practical help in dealing in his court with the customs of a native tribe. Another, who had interested himself in the writings of Elliot Smith and Perry, was firmly convinced that a study of anthropology could be of no practical use to him in spite of its interest. An officer of one of the African colonies who was specially sent to give advice on methods of colonial administration to one of the British Dominions, was asked if it would be a good thing to give a training in anthropology to those who would ultimately become district officers. He replied that it would be useless or even harmful; that a magistrate so trained would be thinking about the shape of a witness's head instead of attending to the evidence he was giving in court. These are typical examples of the sort of thing I have met with over and over again. For the man in the street anthropology is the study of skulls or stone implements or of the ethnological specimens that we collect in our museums, or else theories about the travels of ancient

Egyptians round the world in search of pearls. And indeed, if he judges by the subject as treated in universities, or by the contents of anthropological periodicals, or the proceedings of anthropological congresses, these things do constitute the major part of what is known under the name.

I do not wish for a moment to suggest that these studies are not of academic and scientific value. I am only saying that they are of no value in the practical business of governing and educating dependent peoples. On the other hand, I have been experimenting for ten years with a course of study which consists of a general course covering the whole field of comparative sociology, followed by a functional sociological study of the culture with which the students were to be concerned (Bantu Africa in one instance, New Guinea and Melanesia in another), supplemented by a comparative study of methods and policies of colonial administration and native education considered in the light of the results of comparative sociology. I have found good evidence that such a course of study pursued over not less than one year is really adapted to the needs of the students, and does do what it is claimed anthropology should do, namely, provide a scientific basis for the control and education of native peoples.

In this Empire of ours, in which we have assumed control over so many diverse native peoples in Africa, Asia, Oceania and America, it seems to me that two things are urgently needed if we are to carry out as we should the duties we have thus taken upon ourselves. We have exterminated some of these native peoples and have done, and are doing, irretrievable damage to others. Our injustices, which are many, have been largely the effect of ignorance. One thing, therefore, that is urgently needed is some provision for the systematic study of the native peoples of the Empire. I have pointed out how rapidly material that is of inestimable value for the scientific study of mankind is disappearing through the destruction or modification of backward cultures. From the practical point of view of colonial administration a thorough systematic knowledge of native cultures is required before administration and education can be placed on a sound basis. Research of this kind has been all too long neglected. It can, of course, only be carried out effectively by trained experts. But even if we can find enthusiastic students to take up the difficult and unremunerative work, there is no such provision for research as there is in other sciences. A little, really a very little, considering the magnitude of the work, has been done from our universities, but I am afraid that most of our British universities will not be likely to take any real active interest in the subject until it will be too late to do the work that is now waiting to be done. The International Institute of African Languages and Cultures is preparing to undertake a five-years' program of research in Africa, which I hope will be continued and extended. But for such work we still have to rely on occasional contributions of funds, most of which come from the United States. I feel sometimes ashamed that the great British Empire has to go begging to America for the few hundreds of pounds with which to carry out a little of that work which it is the primary duty of the Empire to undertake if it is ever to rule its dependent peoples with justice based on knowledge and understanding.

I find it difficult to understand how it is that the study of native peoples of simpler culture receives so little support. There seems to be little difficulty in raising very considerable sums of money every year for archaeological investigations. Yet there is no such urgency about these as there is for the immediate study of the living cultures that are being destroyed by the encroachment of the white man. However interesting these dead cultures may be, we study only their dead remains. We can learn very little about their thoughts and feelings, their laws, customs, religion or mythology such as we still can learn about the natives of Africa or New Guinea. At a time, not so long ago, when it would have been possible to observe a people such as the Australian aborigines or the Bushmen making and using stone implements of palaeolithic type, prehistorians were spending their time speculating as to how the very similar Mousterian and Aurignacian implements might have been used.

A second urgent need at the present time seems to me to be the making of further provision for the application of anthropological knowledge to the problems of the government and education of native peoples. I do not think that anyone would maintain that the provision at present made is anything like adequate.

There has been lately some talk of an Institute of Colonial Studies which would be at the same time a centre for research and for making the results of that research available for those engaged in administrative work. I can only express the hope that before many years it will be possible to bring some plan of that kind to completion.

Meanwhile, in spite of repeated setbacks and disappointments, anthropology has at last succeeded in winning for itself some place in the world of practical affairs, some measure of recognition as a study that can make most valuable contributions to problems that are going to be amongst the most important with which this century is faced, those that have arisen from the mingling of diverse peoples and cultures all over the world. The task of the twentieth and succeeding centuries is that of uniting all the peoples of the world in some sort of ordered community. Attention has quite naturally been concentrated on the relations of the great nations. But the problems of finding the proper place in a world community for the tribes of Africa, Asia and Oceania are possibly not less vital to the successful completion of the task.

Chapter IV

MEANING AND SCOPE OF
SOCIAL ANTHROPOLOGY[1]

The name "social anthropology" came into use some sixty years ago to distinguish the subject from ethnology. The avowed aim has always been to apply the inductive method of the natural sciences to the study of human society, its institutions and its evolution. But it is only gradually that we can learn how to apply the inductive method in a new field. The history of chemistry from the time of Bacon to Lavoisier illustrates this. So social anthropology is not now what it was in 1890. At that time theoretical discussions in social anthropology were largely concerned with speculations about origins (of religion, of totemism, of exogamy, etc.). There are still some social anthropologists who remain faithful to the ideas and methods of 1890. But the work now being done in the subject consists largely of experimental studies, combining observation and analysis, of particular social systems, intended to provide material for the systematic comparison of systems of different types and to test existing hypothetical conceptions. Anyone who wants to know what social anthropology is doing at the present day should read the admirable work of Arensberg and Kimball on "Family and Community in Ireland."

One of the most completely organized departments of anthropology is that of the University of Chicago. The subject is divided into five fields: physical anthropology, archaeology, ethnology, linguistics and social anthropol-

[1] *Nature*, CLIV, No. 3904 (August 26, 1944), 257–60.

ogy. Students, who must already have the degree of B.A. before entering the department, are required to devote a period of study to all five subjects and pass a comprehensive examination in all of them. Thereafter the student specializes in one of the fields for his degree of Ph.D. A brilliant student can complete this work in four years, but many take longer.

We may consider this combination of subjects from the point of view of each one of them in turn. Physical anthropology proper, as distinct from human biology, is the study of variation in the human family (the Hominidae) and of human evolution. It includes, therefore, not only the study of existing varieties of *Homo sapiens*, but also human and primate palaeontology. A student who aims at being a competent physical anthropologist must first obtain a thorough grounding in biology, comparative morphology (particularly of the primates), human anatomy, histology, embryology and physiology. It seems desirable that he should have some acquaintance with archaeology and ethnology. His own special work will in no way be helped by any study of linguistics or social anthropology.

Ethnology, as the name shows, is the study of "peoples." Peoples, or ethnic groups, differ from and resemble one another in racial character, in language and in culture. The ethnologist compares and classifies peoples on the bases of these similarities and differences, so that he has to deal with racial, linguistic and cultural classifications. Further, he seeks to discover by various methods something about migrations, interactions and developments of peoples in the past.

It is evident that the competent ethnologist should possess a sound knowledge of physical anthropology, linguistics and social anthropology. Ethnological literature is very heavily overloaded with uncritical speculations. A writer who talks glibly of brachycephaly and dolichocephaly but is completely ignorant of the complexities of structure of the skull will offer us an account of the movements and developments of races from the first appearance of man. One who is ignorant of linguistic science will affirm a connexion of two widely separated languages on the evidence of similarities of a few words selected from imperfect vocabularies. Or one who, by his lack of knowledge of social anthropology, is ignorant of the nature of institutions such as totemism or exogamous moieties, will affirm that these institutions all over the world must have been introduced by Egyptians looking for gold, pearls and cowrie shells.

Prehistoric archaeology is really one kind of ethnology (palaeo-ethnology), the study of the peoples of the prehistoric past who are known to us only from their remains—their dwelling sites, their bones, the implements they made and used. Since the archaeologist recovers no traces of the languages or the social institutions of these vanished peoples he has no need, in the pursuance of his own special studies, for any knowledge of linguistics or social anthropology. On the other hand, he has to know something of geology and surveying. It would seem to be most desirable that ethnology and archaeology should keep closely together. They are merely branches of a single study.

Linguistics, the systematic study of language in general, as distinguished from the study of particular languages or groups of languages, is regarded in the United States as one of the fields of anthropology. In England the subject, as a subject, has not yet received recognition except in the School of Oriental [and African] Studies, London. A student who intends to specialize in linguistics does not really need to know anything more about physical anthropology or prehistoric archaeology than ought to be known by every educated person. But there are important connexions of linguistics with ethnology and social anthropology. For example, the ethnological problem of the Aryan people is a linguistic problem as well as an archaeological, racial and cultural problem.

We come finally to social anthropology—the general theoretical study of social institutions—law, religion, political and economic organization, etc. Within his own field of study, the social anthropologist has no use for physical anthropology. If it should ever be proved that racial (that is, biologically inherited) characters influence social institutions or their development, then he would take due note of the fact.

Prehistoric archaeology obviously makes no contribution to such branches of social anthropology as comparative religion, the comparative study of law or of kinship or of economic systems. It does not even provide very much help to the study of comparative technology as that is conducted in social anthropology, where what is sought is to determine the mutual interrelations between the system of techniques and the other parts of the total social system. Certainly a social anthropologist should be acquainted with the general results of prehistoric archaeology, but the methods of the archaeologist and the details of investigation are not his concern as a social anthropologist.

There is often a good deal of confusion about the relation of social anthropology to ethnology. To a certain extent, but only to a certain extent, they deal with the same facts. But they deal with them in quite different ways. A typical problem of ethnology is how and when the ancestors of the American Indians entered the continent of America and how they developed the differences of racial character, language and culture which they exhibited when Europeans first came in contact with them. A typical problem of social anthropology is, "What is the nature of Law?" An ethnologist and a social anthropologist might both study the same American Indian tribe, but one would be looking for facts relevant to his aim of placing the tribe within his general picture of the peoples of the continent; the other would be examining the way in which the tribe deals with infractions of custom in its bearing on a general theory of the nature and function of law.

Since both ethnology and social anthropology need field studies, there is an obvious economy of labour if a field worker can provide the material needed by the ethnologist and also that needed by the social anthropologist. In some field studies this has been done. But a field study in social anthropology needs more than description; it requires theoretical analysis. There are innumerable examples of ethnographic monographs which are admirable for the purposes of ethnology but are extremely unsatisfactory to the social anthropologist who might wish to make use of the data.

Ethnographical field studies are generally confined to the pre-literate peoples. In the last ten years, field studies by social anthropologists have been carried out on a town in Massachusetts, a town in Mississippi, a French Canadian community, County Clare in Ireland, villages in Japan and China. Such studies of communities in "civilized" countries, carried out by trained investigators, will play an increasingly large part in the social anthropology of the future.

It is now possible to see that what holds the various branches of anthropology together is the central position of ethnology (with archaeology) as the geographical, historical and classificatory study of races and peoples, past and present. It is for this reason that ethnology and anthropology are sometimes regarded as being one and the same. It is an interesting fact that the symposium (as it is now commonly called) on the future of anthropology at the centenary meeting of the Royal Anthropological Institute included discussions of physical anthropology, archaeology, social anthropology and the study of material culture. There was no one to speak on the future of ethnology. Ethnology takes contributions from physical anthropology and linguistics, but gives little to them in return. Social anthropology as the study of evolution is in bad odour with some ethnologists at present, so that while they give little they also take little.

But what of the relations of the branches of anthropology to subjects that lie outside the field of anthropology? Physical anthropology has its closest connexion with the biological sciences. There is a tendency to seek to absorb it into a wider study of human biology, which would, presumably, also include what is called social biology. The study of the Bantu languages or the languages of the American Indians is left to the anthropologist, but not the study of the Indo-European and Semitic languages. How (and why) draw a line between prehistoric archaeology and the archaeology of historic times? But if no such line is drawn, archaeology becomes continuous with history. Ethnology, or some part of it, is claimed as a subdivision of geography—ethnogeography. And where, at the present time, are we to put anthropo-geography or human geography, in geography or in anthropology or in both?

Ethnology deals with the history of peoples. But the rest of history is excluded from anthropology. Yet the closest connexion of social anthropology is with the history of institutions—economic history, the history of religion, of law, of political organization, of science, etc. But to the social anthropologist the history of Europe or of Christianity is of no more interest than the history of India or China, of Islam or Buddhism.

The writer of the article on "The Future of Anthropology" (see *Nature*, Nov. 20, 1943, p. 587), which surveyed the discussion at the centenary meeting of the Royal Anthropological Institute, asks, "Who is to study the world-wide history and development of social institutions?" The answer is, in the first place, the historians. The social anthropologist cannot examine for himself the original sources for the economic, political, legal and religious history of ancient Greece and Rome, India, China, Russia, Persia and Turkey. It is unusual for him to be thoroughly competent in even one of these fields. The social anthropologist, for the most part, has to take the facts about institutional history and development from the historians, though, of course, he has to exercise his judgment as to the reliability of a particular historian. What the social anthropologist does with this material is to use it to formulate his general hypotheses about law, religion, economic organization and so on. But these hypotheses need to be verified; and although some verification is possible by the comparison of different historical societies, the final test lies in actual (experimental) observation of existing social systems.

Political systems, economic systems, and systems of law are studied in social anthropology and also in economics, political science and jurisprudence. But there are very important differences of method. One of these, though by no means the most important, is that in the three studies mentioned attention is usually confined to certain types of society, whereas social anthropology has for its field all human societies and therefore tends to pay most attention to those which are neglected by the social sciences. It is true that at present there is no close connexion of the three social sciences with social anthropology, but this may be expected to develop as the last-named subject itself develops.

As anthropology is at present recognized, psychology lies outside. Yet social anthropology stands in a very close relation to psychology. To make the relationship clear it is necessary to distinguish between two kinds of psychology. Psychology is here taken to mean the study of the mental or psychic systems—if you will, the behaviour systems—of organisms. We may study the behaviour, the external manifestations of the psyche, of earthworms, rats or chimpanzees. General human psychology deals with the mental characteristics which are possessed by all human beings. Social anthropology deals with the characteristics of all human social systems. A social system consists of a certain set of social relations between certain human beings, exhibited to observation in their interactions with one another. It is obvious that one determining factor in the formation of human social systems is that basic human nature which it is the business of the general psychologist to study. Similarly, the nature of multicellular organisms is determined by the nature of the living cell which it is the business of the cytologist, the biochemist and the biophysicist to study. The connexion between social anthropology and general psychology is just as close and of just the same kind as the relation between animal physiology and cytology.

There are also what may conveniently be called "special psychologies." These deal, not with the universal characteristics of human beings, with basic human nature, but with the special mental or behaviour characteristics of individuals, types, classes or groups. Psychiatry affords an example of a "special psychology," as do attempts to define psychological "types"—extrovert, introvert; schizophrenic, cyclothymic; pycnic, asthenic.

One of the "special psychologies" consists of the study of the psychical characteristics (that is, characteristics of mind or behaviour) of the members of a defined social group, either a local community or a defined social class within a local community. When we study the "psychology" of the French or the Germans or the people of the United States, we are dealing with those characteristics of mind or behaviour that result from "conditioning" by a particular social system. Here the "special" characteristics with which we are concerned are determined by the social system, while the social system itself is determined by the general characteristics of basic human nature.

It should be evident that there is a two-way connexion between social anthropology and psychology. Human societies are what they are because human beings are what they are. Similarly a human body is what it is because living cells are what they are. But why human beings belonging to a particular society or group exhibit certain characteristic modes of behaviour is because they have been "conditioned," as the phrase is, by that society. Similarly the cells of a muscle act and react as they do because they are individual members of the muscle.

Prof. F. C. Bartlett (*Nature*, Dec. 18, 1943, p. 700) proposes drastic changes. He would give no place in anthropology to archaeology, to linguistics (the general study of language), to ethnology (the geographical and historical study of races and peoples), or to social anthropology (as the comparative study of the forms of association found among human beings or as the study of social evolution). He would retain physical anthropology or anthropometry if it would abandon its present aim of studying evolution, variation and heredity in the human family and would devote itself to measuring physical characters that are correlated with differences of behaviour. He would also admit the study of material culture so long as it was limited to the study of the applications of natural knowledge and their influence on behaviour. He adds two other disciplines. One is the study of the effects of general environmental conditions on behaviour. The other is the study of "a group's psychological possessions, its traditions, beliefs, customs, ideals and of their repercussion upon social conduct." For Prof. Bartlett, anthropology should become a group of special psychologies dealing with the effects on behaviour of anatomical characters, environment, knowledge and the "psychological possessions" of groups. Anthropologists need not fear, however, that Prof. Bartlett's drastic reforms will be carried out in the near future. Meanwhile, that "special psychology" which is concerned with the way in which the behaviour of individuals is determined by the "culture" of the society in which they live is already part of social anthropology. But to say that it should be the whole of it is to deny to social anthropology the right to that study of the nature of social systems and of their evolution which is the *raison d'être* of the science.

Applied social anthropology is not much more than twenty years old. It was developed in South Africa, England and Australia in connexion with problems of Colonial administration. About twelve years ago it secured, despite the opposition of some ethnologists, a footing in the United States, not only in the Indian Bureau but also in the Soil Conservation Bureau and in an investigation of factory efficiency carried out in a large factory under the direction of Prof. Elton Mayo of Harvard. Since the United States came into the war, large numbers of anthropologists have been called to Washington to carry out work which either is, or is supposed to be, applied anthropology.

There is a good deal of misunderstanding about applied anthropology, what it is, what it can do and what it cannot do, but that matter obviously cannot be discussed here. The recognition of applied social anthropology has certain very definite advantages and certain equally definite disadvantages. To mention only one of the latter, theoretical social anthropology is still in the formative stage. The demand on social anthropologists to spend too much of their time on practical problems would inevitably reduce the amount of work that can be given to the development of the theoretical side of the science. But without a sound basis in theory, applied anthropology must deteriorate and become not applied science, but merely empirical practice.

What of the future? Social anthropology must claim a position of relative independence. (There are already chairs of social anthropology at Oxford and Cambridge.) This does not mean that it should sever its connexion with ethnology, with which it has always been associated; and its connexion with ethnology connects it indirectly with prehistoric archaeology. It should maintain a close connexion with general linguistics, for language is a social institution. (At Oxford the only lectures on general linguistics have been those given in the Institute of Social Anthropology.) It could maintain a closer connexion with human biology than with the narrower subject of physical anthropology.

Outside the field of what is called anthropology, it must maintain or establish connexions with psychology, with history (more particularly economic history, the history of law, of political organization, of religion) and with economics, political science and jurisprudence. The history of culture, in the sense of the history of art, of music, of literature, ought not to be neglected in any complete social anthropology nor, of course, technological history. In the training of a social anthropologist the first essential is a real understanding of the experimental method in scientific investigation, and this is best acquired by a thorough study of the history of science.

One part of social anthropology is the comparative study of economic systems. Surely there ought to be close connexion between this study and economics and economic history. Another part of social anthropology is the comparative study of legal systems, which demands a similar connexion with jurisprudence and the history of law; and so on with other parts of social anthropology. But what part of social anthropology would give a similar close connexion with the study of the somatic differences exhibited by the various races of mankind, or with the study of the date and the affinities of the Solutrean or Capsian culture? So long as ethnology continues to exist, it will provide a meeting-ground for archaeologists, physical anthropologists, students of linguistics, and social anthropologists. Such a meeting-ground has been provided for a century by the Royal Anthropological Institute and will continue to be provided in the future. Any attempt to impose a more rigid artificial unity will be likely to produce exactly the opposite of the result at which it aims.

Chapter V

THE COMPARATIVE METHOD IN
SOCIAL ANTHROPOLOGY[1]

What is meant when one speaks of "the comparative method" in anthropology is the method used by such a writer as Frazer in his *Golden Bough*. But comparisons of particular features of social life can be made for either of two very different purposes, which correspond to the distinction now commonly made in England between ethnology and social anthropology. The existence of similar institutions, customs or beliefs in two or more societies may in certain instances be taken by the ethnologist as pointing to some historical connection. What is aimed at is some sort of reconstruction of the history of a society or people or region. In comparative sociology or social anthropology the purpose of comparison is different, the aim being to explore the varieties of forms of social life as a basis for the theoretical study of human social phenomena.

Franz Boas, writing in 1888 and 1896, pointed out that in anthropology there are two tasks to be undertaken. One kind of task is to "reconstruct" the history of particular regions or peoples, and this he spoke of as being "the first task." The second task he describes as follows: "A comparison of the social life of different peoples proves that the foundations of their cultural development are remarkably uniform. It follows from this that there are laws to which this development is subject. Their discovery is the second, perhaps the more important aim of

[1] *Journal of the Royal Anthropological Institute*, LXXXI (1952), 15–22. Huxley Memorial Lecture for 1951.

our science. . . . In the pursuit of these studies we find that the same custom, the same idea, occurs among peoples for whom we cannot establish any historical connection, so that a common historical origin cannot be assumed and it becomes necessary to decide whether there are laws that result in the same, or at least similar, phenomena independently of historical causes. Thus develops the second important task of ethnology, the investigation of the laws governing social life." "The frequent occurrence of similar phenomena in cultural areas that have no historical contact suggests that important results may be obtained from their study, for it shows that the human mind develops everywhere according to the same laws."

Boas included these two tasks in the single discipline which he called sometimes "anthropology," sometimes "ethnology." To some of us in this country it seems more convenient to refer to those investigations that are concerned with the reconstruction of history as belonging to ethnology and to keep the term social anthropology for the study of discoverable regularities in the development of human society in so far as these can be illustrated or demonstrated by the study of primitive peoples.

Thus, the comparative method in social anthropology is the method of those who have been called "arm-chair anthropologists" since they work in libraries. Their first task is to look for what used to be called "parallels," similar social features appearing in different societies, in the present or in the past. At Cambridge sixty years ago Frazer represented arm-chair anthropology using the comparative method, while Haddon urged the need of "intensive" studies of particular societies by systematic field studies of competent observers. The development of field studies has led to a relative neglect of studies making use of the comparative method. This is both understandable and excusable, but it does have some regrettable effects. The student is told that he must consider any feature of social life in its context, in its relation to the other features of the particular social system in which it is found. But he is often not taught to look at it in the wider context of human societies in general. The teaching of the Cambridge school of anthropology forty-five years ago was not that arm-chair anthropology was to be abandoned but that it must be combined with intensive studies of particular primitive societies in which any particular institution, custom, or belief of the society should be examined in relation to the total social system of which it was a part or item. Without systematic comparative studies anthropology will become only historiography and ethnography. Sociological theory must be based on, and continually tested by, systematic comparison.

The only really satisfactory way of explaining a method is by means of illustration. Let us therefore consider how the method can be applied in a particular instance. We may take our start with a particular feature of some tribes in the interior of New South Wales. In these tribes there is a division of the population into two parts, which are named after the eaglehawk and the crow (Kilpara and Makwara). There is a rule by which a man should only take a wife from the division other than his own, and that the children will belong to the same division as their mother. The system is described in technical terms as one of totemically represented exogamous matrilineal moieties.

One way of explaining why a particular society has the features that it does have is by its history. As we have no authentic history of these or other Australian tribes the historical anthropologists are reduced to offering us imaginary histories. Thus the Rev. John Mathew would explain these divisions and their names by supposing that two different peoples, one called Eaglehawks and the other Crows, met in this part of Australia and fought with each other. Ultimately they decided to make peace and agreed that in future Eaglehawk men would only marry Crow women and *vice versa*.

Let us begin looking for parallels. There is a very close parallel to be found amongst the Haida of north-west America, who also have a division into two exogamous matrilineal moieties which are named after the eagle and the raven, two species which correspond very closely indeed to the eaglehawk and crow of Australia. The Haida have a legend that in the beginning only the eagle possessed fresh water which he kept in a basket. The raven discovered this and succeeded in stealing the water from the eagle. But as he flew with the basket over Queen Charlotte Island the water was spilled from the heavy basket and formed the lakes and rivers from which all birds can now drink; and salmon made their way into the streams and now furnish food for men.

In some parts of Australia there are similar legends about the eaglehawk and the crow. One is to the effect that in the beginning only the eaglehawk possessed a supply of fresh water, which he kept under a large stone. The crow, spying on him, saw him lift the stone and take a drink, then replace the stone. The crow proceeded to lift the stone, and after he had taken a drink of fresh water scratched the lice from his head into the water and did not replace the stone. The result was that the water escaped and formed the rivers of eastern Australia in which the lice became the Murray cod that were an important item of food for the aborigines just as salmon are in north-west America. If we accept the criteria formulated by the diffusionists, such as Graebner, we have here what they would say is evidence of a historical connection between Australia and the Pacific coast of North America.

Once we begin looking for parallels to the eaglehawk-crow division of Australia we find many instances of exogamous moieties, in some instances matrilineal, in others patrilineal, in the rest of Australia, and frequently the divisions are named after or represented by birds. In Victoria we find black cockatoo and white cockatoo, in Western Australia white cockatoo and crow. In New Ireland there is a similar system in which the moieties are associated with the sea-eagle and the fish-hawk. At this point we may feel inclined to ask why these social divisions should be identified by reference to two species of birds.

In Eastern Australia the division of the population into two sexes is represented by what is called sex totemism. In tribes of New South Wales the men have for their "brother" the bat, and the women have for their "sister" the night owl in some tribes and the owlet nightjar in others. In the northern part of New South Wales the totems are the bat for men and the tree-creeper for women. (It must be remembered that the Australian aborigines classify the bat as a "bird.") So we find another dichotomy of society in which the divisions are represented by birds.

Throughout most of Australia there is a very important social division into two alternating generation divisions or endogamous moieties. One division consists of all the persons of a single generation together with those of the generation of their grandparents and the generation of their grandchildren, while the other division includes all those of the generation of their parents and the generation of their children. These divisions are rarely given names but in some tribes may be referred to by terms, one of which a man applies to his own division and its members while the other is applied to the other division. But in one part of Western Australia these endogamous moieties are named after the kingfisher and the bee-eater, while in another part they are named after a little red bird and a little black bird.

Our question "Why all these birds?" is thus widened in its scope. It is not only the exogamous moieties, but also dual divisions of other kinds that are identified by connection with a pair of birds. It is, however, not always a question of birds. In Australia the moieties may be associated with other pairs of animals, with two species of kangaroo in one part, with two species of bee in another. In California one moiety is associated with the coyote and the other with the wild cat.

Our collection of parallels could be extended to other instances in which a social group or division is given an identity and distinguished from others by association with a natural species. The Australian moieties are merely one instance of a widely spread social phenomenon. From the particular phenomenon we are led, by the comparative method, to a much more general problem—How can we understand the customs by which social groups and divisions are distinguished by associating a particular group or division with a particular natural species? This is the general problem of totemism, as it has been designated. I do not offer you a solution of this problem, as it seems to me to be the resultant of two other problems. One is the problem of the way in which in a particular society the relation of human beings to natural species is represented, and as a contribution to this problem I have offered an analysis of the non-totemic Andaman Islanders. The other is the problem of how social groups come to be identified by connection with some emblem, symbol, or object having symbolic or emblematic reference. A nation identified by its flag, a family identified by its coat of arms, a particular congregation of a church identified by its relation to a particular saint, a clan identified by its relation to a totemic species; these are all so many examples of a single class of phenomena for which we have to look for a general theory.

The problem to which it is desired to draw your attention here is a different one. Granted that is is for some reason appropriate to identify social divisions by association with natural species, what is the principle by which such pairs as eaglehawk and crow, eagle and raven, coyote and wild cat are chosen as representing the moieties of a dual division? The reason for asking this question is not idle curiosity. We may, it can be held, suppose that an understanding of the principle in question will give us an important insight into the way in which the natives themselves think about the dual division as a part of their social structure. In other words, instead of asking "Why all these birds?" we can ask "Why particularly eaglehawk and crow, and other pairs?"

I have collected many tales about Eaglehawk and Crow in different parts of Australia, and in all of them the two are represented as opponents in some sort of conflict. A single example must suffice and it comes from Western Australia. Eaglehawk was the mother's brother of Crow. In these tribes a man marries the daughter of a mother's brother so that Eaglehawk was the possible father-in-law of Crow, to whom therefore he owed obligations such as that of providing him with food. Eaglehawk told his nephew to go and hunt wallaby. Crow, having killed a wallaby, ate it himself, an extremely reprehensible action in terms of native morality. On his return to the camp his uncle asked him what he had brought, and Crow, being a liar, said that he had succeeded in getting nothing. Eaglehawk then said, "But what is in your belly, since your hunger-belt is no longer tight?" Crow replied that to stay the pangs of hunger he had filled his belly with the gum from the acacia. The uncle replied that he did not believe him and would tickle him until he vomited. (This incident

is given in the legend in the form of a song of Eaglehawk—
Balmanangabalu ngabarina, kidji-kidji malidyala.) The
crow vomited the wallaby that he had eaten. Thereupon
Eaglehawk seized him and rolled him in the fire; his eyes
became red with the fire, he was blackened by the char-
coal, and he called out in pain "Wa! Wa! Wa!" Eaglehawk pronounced what was to be the law "You will never
be a hunter, but you will for ever be a thief." And that is
how things now are.

To interpret this tale we have to consider how these
birds appear to the aborigines. In the first place they are
the two chief meat-eating birds and the Australian abo-
rigine thinks of himself as a meat-eater. One method of
hunting in this region is for a number of men and women
to come together at an an appropriate season for a collective hunt. A fire across a stretch of country is started in
such a way that it will be spread by the wind. The men
advance in front of the fire killing with spear or throwing
stick the animals that are fleeing from it, while the women
follow the fire to dig out such animals as bandicoots that
have taken refuge underground. When such a hunt has
been started it will not be long before first one and then
another eaglehawk makes its appearance to join in the
hunting of the animals in flight from the advancing flames.
Eaglehawk is the hunter.

The crow does not join in this or any other kind of
hunt, but when a camp fire is started it is rarely very long
before a crow makes his appearance to settle in a tree out
of reach of a throwing stick and wait for the chance of
thieving a piece of meat for his dinner.

Amongst the tales told by the Australians about animals we can find an immense number of parallels to this
tale of Eaglehawk and Crow. Here, as an example, is one
about the wombat and the kangaroo from the region
where South Australia adjoins Victoria. In this region the

wombat and the kangaroo are the two largest meat animals. In the beginning Wombat and Kangaroo lived together as friends. One day Wombat began to make a "house" for himself. (The wombat lives in a burrow in the ground.) Kangaroo jeered at him and thus annoyed him. Then one day it rained. (It is to be remembered that in these tales whatever happens is thought of as happening for the first time in the history of the world.) Wombat went into his "house" out of the rain. Kangaroo asked Wombat to make room for him, but the latter explained that there was only room for one. Thus Wombat and Kangaroo quarrelled and fought. Kangaroo hit Wombat on the head with a big stone, flattening his skull; Wombat threw a spear at Kangaroo which fixed itself at the base of the backbone. The wombat has a flattened skull to this day and the kangaroo has a tail; the former lives in a burrow while the kangaroo lives in the open; they are no longer friends.

This is, of course, a "just-so" story which you may think is childish. It amuses the listeners when it is told with the suitable dramatic expressions. But if we examine some dozens of these tales we find that they have a single theme. The resemblances and differences of animal species are translated into terms of friendship and conflict, solidarity and opposition. In other words the world of animal life is represented in terms of social relations similar to those of human society.

One may find legends which relate not to particular species or pairs of species but to animals in general. There is a legend in New South Wales according to which in the beginning all the animals formed a single society. Then the bat was responsible for introducing death into the world by killing his two wives. His brothers-in-law called all the animals to a corroborree, and catching the bat unawares threw him into the fire. This started a general fight in which the animals attacked each other with fire, and of this fight all the animals now show the marks. The various species no longer form one society of friends.

There is a very similar tale in the Andaman Islands. The various species of animals originally formed a single society. At a meeting one of them brought fire. There was a general quarrel in which they all threw fire at each other. Some fled into the sea and became fishes, others escaped into the trees and became birds, and birds and fishes still show the marks of the burns they suffered.

A comparative study therefore reveals to us the fact that the Australian ideas about the eaglehawk and the crow are only a particular instance of a widespread phenomenon. First, these tales interpret the resemblances and differences of animal species in terms of social relationships of friendship and antagonism as they are known in the social life of human beings. Secondly, natural species are placed in pairs of opposites. They can only be so regarded if there is some respect in which they resemble each other. Thus eaglehawk and crow resemble each other in being the two prominent meat-eating birds. When I first investigated the sex totems of New South Wales I supposed, quite wrongly, that what was the basic resemblance of the bat and the night owl or nightjar was that they both fly about at night. But the tree-creeper does not fly at night and is the totem of the women in the northern part of New South Wales. As I was sitting in the region of the Macleay River with a native a tree-creeper made its appearance, and I asked him to tell me about it. "That is the bird that taught women how to climb trees" he told me. After some conversation I asked "What resemblance is there between the bat and the tree-creeper?" and with an expression on his face that showed surprise that I should ask such a question he replied, "But of course they both live in holes in trees." I realised that the night owl and the nightjar also live in trees. The fact that certain animals eat meat constitutes a sort of social similarity, as of eaglehawk and crow or dingo and wild cat. Similarly the habit of living in holes in trees.

We can now answer the question "Why eaglehawk and crow?" by saying that these are selected as representing a certain kind of relationship which we may call one of "opposition."

The Australian idea of what is here called "opposition" is a particular application of that association by contrariety that is a universal feature of human thinking, so that we think by pairs of contraries, upwards and downwards, strong and weak, black and white. But the Australian conception of "opposition" combines the idea of a pair of contraries with that of a pair of opponents. In the tales about eaglehawk and crow the two birds are opponents in the sense of being antagonists. They are also contraries by reason of their difference of character, Eaglehawk the hunter, Crow the chief. Black cockatoo and white cockatoo which represent the moieties in Western Victoria are another example of contrariety, the birds being essentially similar except for the contrast of colour. In America the moieties are referred to by other pairs of contraries, Heaven and Earth, war and peace, up-stream and down-stream, red and white. After a lengthy comparative study I think I am fully justified in stating a general law, that wherever, in Australia, Melanesia or America, there exists a social structure of exogamous moieties, the moieties are thought of as being in a relation of what is here called "opposition."

Obviously the next step in a comparative study is to attempt to discover what are the various forms that the opposition between the moieties of a dual division takes in actual social life. In the literature there are occasional references to a certain hostility between the two divisions described as existing or reported to have existed in the past. All the available evidence is that there is no real hostility in the proper sense of the term but only a conventional attitude which finds expression in some customary mode of behaviour. Certainly in Australia, although in some instances where there is a dispute it is possible to observe the members of the two patrilineal moieties forming separate "sides," real hostility, of the kind that may lead to violent action is not between the moieties but between local groups, and two local groups of the same patrilineal moiety seem to be just as frequently in conflict as two groups belonging to different moieties. Indeed, since a common source of actual conflict is the taking by one man of a woman married to or betrothed to another the two antagonists or groups of antagonists in such instances will both belong to the same patrilineal moiety.

The expression of opposition between the moieties may take various forms. One is the institution to which anthropologists have given the not very satisfactory name of "the joking relationship." Members of opposite divisions are permitted or expected to indulge in teasing each other, in verbal abuse or in exchange of insults. Kroeber (*Handbook of Indians of California*) writes that amongst the Cupeño "a sort of good natured opposition is recognized between the moieties, whose members frequently taunt each other with being unsteady and slow-witted, respectively." Strong (*Aboriginal Society in Southern California*) reports the same thing. "A good-natured antagonism between the moieties exhibits itself in joking between persons of the one and the other. The coyote people taunt the wild cat people with being slow-witted and lazy like their animal representative and the wild cat people retaliate by accusing their opponents with being unsteady. There are indications that this teasing of one moiety by another entered into their serious ceremonies. There were songs of a satirical kind that could be sung by one moiety against the other. However, the opposition between the moieties seems to have been much less strong than between certain pairs of clans, sometimes belonging to the same moiety, which were traditionally 'enemies.' These clans, on certain occasions, would sing 'enemy songs' against each other."

This institution, for which it is to be hoped that some one will find a better name than "joking relationship," is found in a variety of forms in a number of different societies, and calls for systematic comparative study. It has for its function to maintain a continuous relationship between two persons, or two groups, of apparent but factitious hostility or antagonism. I have offered a suggestion towards a comparative study of this institution in a paper published in the journal *Africa*.[2]

Another significant custom in which is expressed the relation of opposition between the two moieties is that by which, in some tribes of Australia and in some of North America the moieties provide the "sides" in games such as football. Competitive games provide a social occasion on which two persons or two groups of persons are opponents. Two continuing groups in a social structure can be maintained in a relation in which they are regularly opponents. An example is provided by the two universities of Oxford and Cambridge.

There are other customs in which the opposition of moieties is expressed. For example, in the Omaha tribe of North America the camp circle was divided into two semicircles, and when a boy of the one half crossed into the other he took companions with him and there was a fight with the boys of the other moiety. We need not and can not here examine these various customs.

[2] See *Africa*, XIII, No. 3 (1940), 195–210. Reprinted in *Structure and Function in Primitive Society* (London, 1952). See also *Africa*, XIX (1949), 133–40.

Let us consider briefly the institution of moiety exogamy, by which every marriage, where the rule is observed, is between persons belonging to opposite moieties. There are innumerable customs which show that in many primitive societies the taking of a woman in marriage is represented symbolically as an act of hostility against her family or group. Every anthropologist is familiar with the custom by which it is represented that the bride is captured or taken by force from her kinsfolk. A first collection of instances of this custom was made by McLennan who interpreted them historically as being survivals from the earliest condition of human society in which the only way to obtain a wife was to steal or capture a woman from another tribe.

An illuminating example of this kind of custom is provided by the people of the Marquesas. When a marriage has been arranged the kinsmen of the bridegroom take the gifts which are to be offered to the kinsfolk of the bride and proceed towards the bride's home. On the way they are ambushed and attacked by the bride's kin who seize by force the goods that they are conveying. The first act of violence comes from the kin of the bride. By the Polynesian principle of *utu* those who suffer an injury are entitled to retaliate by inflicting an injury. So the bridegroom's kinsmen exercise this right by carrying off the bride. No example could better illustrate the fact that these customary actions are symbolic.

Viewed in relation to social structure the meaning or symbolic reference of these customs ought to be obvious. The solidarity of a group requires that the loss of one of its members shall be recognized as an injury to the group. Some expression of this is therefore called for. The taking of a woman in marriage is represented as in some sense an act of hostility against her kin. This is what is meant by the saying of the Gusii of East Africa "Those whom we marry are those whom we fight."

It is in the light of this that we must interpret the custom of marriage by exchange. The group or kin of a woman lose her when she marries; they are compensated for their loss if they receive another who will become the wife of one of them. In Australian tribes, with a few exceptions, the custom is that when a man takes a wife he should give a sister to replace her. In the Yaralde tribe of South Australia, which did not have a system of moieties, when a man married a woman of another local clan, his own clan was expected to provide a wife for some member of the clan from which the bride came. Otherwise the marriage was regarded as irregular, improper, or we might almost say illegal. It has been reported from the tribes of the eastern part of Victoria (Gippsland) that the only proper form of marriage was by exchange. The system of exogamous moieties provides a system of generalisation of marriage by exchange, since every marriage is one incident in the continual process by which the men of one moiety get their wives from the other.

A comparative study shows that in many primitive societies the relation established between two groups of kin by a marriage between a man of one group and a woman of the other is one which is expressed by customs of avoidance and by the joking relationship. In many societies a man is required to avoid any close social contact with the mother of his wife, frequently also with her father, and with other persons of that generation amongst his wife's kin. With this custom there is frequently associated the custom called the "joking relationship" by which a man is permitted or even required to use insulting behaviour to some of his wife's kin of his own generation. I have elsewhere suggested that these customs can be understood as being the conventional means by which a relationship of a peculiar kind, which can be described as a compound of friendship or solidarity with hostility or opposition is established and maintained.

In a complete study there are other features of the dual organization that would need to be taken into consideration. There are instances in which there are regular exchanges of goods or services between the two moieties. In that competitive exchange of food and valuables known as "potlatch" in North America, the moieties may be significant. Amongst the Tlingit, for example, it is members of one moiety who potlatch against members of the other moiety. The two moieties provide the "sides" for what is a sort of competitive game in which men "fight with property."

Our comparative study enables us to see the eaglehawk-crow division of the Darling River tribes as one particular example of a widespread type of the application of a certain structural principle. The relation between the two divisions, which has here been spoken of by the term "opposition" is one which separates and also unites, and which therefore gives us a rather special kind of social integration which deserves systematic study. But the term "opposition" which I have been obliged to use because I cannot find a better, is not wholly appropriate, for it stresses too much what is only one side of the relationship, that of separation and difference. The more correct description would be to say that the kind of structure with which we are concerned is one of the union of opposites.

The idea of a unity of contraries was one of the leading ideas of the philosophy of Heraclitus. It is summed up in his statement, "Polemos is king, rules all things." The Greek word *polemos* is sometimes translated as "strife," but the appropriate translation would be "opposition" in the sense in which that word has been used in this lecture. Heraclitus uses as one example the mortise and the tenon; these are not at strife; they are contraries or opposites which combine to make a unity when they are joined together.

There is some evidence that this idea of the union of

opposites was derived by Heraclitus and the Pythagoreans from the East. At any rate the most complete elaboration of the idea is to be found in the Yin-Yang philosophy of ancient China. The phrase in which this is summed up is "*Yi yin yi yang wei tze tao.*" One yin and one yang make an order. Yin is the feminine principle, Yang the masculine. The word "tao" can here be best translated as "an ordered whole." One man (yang) and his wife (yin) constitute the unity of a married couple. One day (yang) and one night (yin) make a unified whole or unity of time, Similarly one summer (yang) and one winter (yin) make up the unity we call a year. Activity is yang and passivity is yin and a relation of two entities or persons of which one is active and the other passive is also conceived as a unity of opposites. In this ancient Chinese philosophy this idea of the unity of opposites is given the widest possible extension. The whole universe including human society is interpreted as an "order" based on this.

There is historical evidence that this philosophy was developed many centuries ago in the region of the Yellow River, the "Middle Kingdom." There is also evidence that the social organization of this region was one of paired intermarrying clans, the two clans meeting together at the Spring and Autumn Festivals, and competing in the singing of odes, so that the men of the one clan could find wives amongst the daughters of the other. The evidence is that the system of marriage was one where a man married his mother's brother's daughter, or a woman of the appropriate generation of his mother's clan. According to my information this kind of organization, which apparently existed forty centuries ago in that region, still survived there in 1935, but the investigation of it that I had planned to be carried out by Li Yu I was unfortunately prevented by the Japanese attack on China. It may still not be too late for this to be done; it would

enable us to evaluate more exactly the historical reconstruction of Marcel Granet.

This Yin-Yang philosophy of ancient China is the systematic elaboration of the principle that can be used to
define the social structure of moieties in Australian tribes,
for the structure of moieties is, as may be seen from the
brief account here given, one of a unity of opposing
groups, in the double sense that the two groups are
friendly opponents, and that they are represented as being
in some sense opposites, in the way in which eaglehawk
and crow or black and white are opposites.

Light can be thrown on this by the consideration of
another instance of opposition in Australian societies. An
Australian camp includes men of a certain local clan and
their wives who, by the rule of exogamy, have come from
other clans. In New South Wales there is a system of sex
totemism, by which one animal species is the "brother" of
the men, and another species is the "sister" of the wom-
en. Occasionally there arises within a native camp a condition of tension between the sexes. What is then likely to
happen, according to the accounts of the aborigines, is
that the women will go out and kill a bat, the "brother" or
sex totem of the men, and leave it lying in the camp for the
men to see. The men then retaliate by killing the bird
which in that tribe is the sex totem of the women. The
women then utter abuse against the men and this leads to
a fight with sticks (digging sticks for the women, throwing
sticks for the men) between the two sex groups in which a
good many bruises are inflicted. After the fight peace is
restored and the tension is eliminated. The Australian
aborigines have the idea that where there is a quarrel between two persons or two groups which is likely to smoul-
der the thing to do is for them to fight it out and then
make friends. The symbolic use of the totem is very significant. This custom shows us that the idea of the opposition of groups, and the union of opposites is not con-

fined to the exogamous moieties. The two sex groups provide a structure of a similar kind; so sometimes do the two groups formed by the alternating generation divisions. The group of the fathers, and the group of their sons are in a relation of opposition, not dissimilar from the relation between husbands and their wives.

We can say that in the relatively simple social structure of Australian tribes we can recognize three principal types of relationship between persons or groups. There is the relationship of enmity and strife; at the other extreme there is the relationship of simple solidarity, and in the Australian system this ought to exist between brothers, and between persons of the same generation in the local group; such persons may not fight, though in certain circumstances it is thought to be legitimate for one person to "growl" against the other, to express in the camp a complaint against the action of the other. There is thirdly the relationship of opposition, which is not at all the same thing as strife or enmity, but is a combination of agreement and disagreement, of solidarity and difference.

We began with a particular feature of a particular region in Australia, the existence of exogamous moieties named after the eaglehawk and the crow. By making comparisons amongst other societies, some of them not Australian, we are enabled to see that this is not something particular or peculiar to one region, but is one instance of certain widespread general tendencies in human societies. We thus substitute for a particular problem of the kind that calls for a historical explanation, certain general problems. There is, for example, the problem of totemism as a social phenomenon in which there is a special association of a social group with a natural species. Another, and perhaps more important, problem that has been raised, is that of the nature and functioning of social relationships and social structures based on what has here been called "opposition." This is a much more general problem than that of totemism for it is the problem of how opposition can be used as a mode of social integration. The comparative method is therefore one by which we pass from the particular to the general, from the general to the more general, with the end in view that we may in this way arrive at the universal, at characteristics which can be found in different forms in all human societies.

But the comparative method does not only formulate problems, though the formulation of the right problems is extremely important in any science; it also provides material by which the first steps may be made towards the solution. A study of the system of moieties in Australia can give us results that should have considerable value for the theory of human society.

At the beginning of this lecture I quoted Franz Boas as having distinguished two tasks with which an anthropologist can concern himself in the study of primitive society, and these two tasks call for two different methods. One is the "historical" method, by which the existence of a particular feature in a particular society is "explained" as the result of a particular sequence of events. The other is the comparative method by which we seek, not to "explain," but to understand a particular feature of a particular society by first seeing it as a particular instance of a general kind or class of social phenomena, and then by relating it to a certain general, or preferably a universal, tendency in human societies. Such a tendency is what is called in certain instances a law. Anthropology as the study of primitive society includes both methods, and I have myself consistently used both in the teaching of ethnology and social anthropology in a number of universities. But there must be discrimination. The historical method will give us particular propositions, only the comparative method can give us general propositions. In primitive societies historical evidence is always lacking or inadequate. There is no historical evidence as to how the eaglehawk-crow division in Australia came into existence, and guesses about it seem to me of no significance whatever. How the Australian aborigines arrived at their present social systems is, and forever must be, entirely unknown. The supposition that by the comparative method we might arrive at valid conclusions about the "origins" of those systems shows a complete disregard for the nature of historical evidence. Anthropology, as the study of primitive societies, includes both historical (ethnographical and ethnological) studies and also the generalizing study known as social anthropology which is a special branch of comparative sociology. It is desirable that the aims and methods should be distinguished. History, in the proper sense of the term, as an authentic account of the succession of events in a particular region over a particular period of time, cannot give us generalizations. The comparative method as a generalising study of the features of human societies cannot give us particular histories. The two studies can only be combined and adjusted when their difference is properly recognized and it is for this reason that thirty years ago I urged that there should be a clear distinction between ethnology as the historical study of primitive societies and social anthropology as that branch of comparative sociology that concerns itself specially with the societies we call primitive. We can leave all questions of historical reconstruction to ethnology. For social anthropology the task is to formulate and validate statements about the conditions of existence of social systems (laws of social statics) and the regularities that are observable in social change (laws of social dynamics). This can only be done by the systematic use of the comparative method, and the only justification of that method is the expectation that it will provide us with results of this kind, or, as Boas stated it, will provide us with knowledge of the laws of social development. It will be only in an integrated and organized study in which historical studies and sociological studies are combined that we shall be able to reach a real understanding of the development of human society, and this we do not yet have.

PART II

SOCIAL ANTHROPOLOGY

Chapter I

DEFINITION

Social anthropology may be defined as the investigation of the nature of human society by the systematic comparison of societies of diverse types, with particular attention to the simpler forms of society of primitive, savage or non-literate peoples. The name came into use in England in the last quarter of the nineteenth century and has received recognition in the British universities, in some of which there are now professorships and lectureships in social anthropology. It was adopted in order to distinguish the subject from ethnology on the one hand and from what had come to be known as sociology on the other.

The first person to have the title of Professor of Social Anthropology was Sir James Frazer, who was given an honorary professorship in the University of Liverpool in 1908. In his inaugural lecture on "The Scope of Social Anthropology," delivered on May 14, 1908, he said:

Anthropology in the widest sense of the word, aims at discovering the general laws which have regulated human history in the past, and which, if nature is really uniform, may be expected to regulate it in the future. Hence the science of man coincides to a certain extent with what has long been known as the philosophy of history as well as with the study to which of late years the name of Sociology has been given. Indeed it might with some reason be held that Social Anthropology, or the study of man in society, is only another expression for Sociology. Yet I think that the two sciences may be conveniently distinguished, and that while the name of Sociology should be reserved for the study of human society in the most comprehensive sense of the words, the name of Social Anthropology may with advantage be restricted to one particular department of that immense field of knowledge. . . . The sphere of Social Anthropology as I understand it, or at least as I propose to treat it, is limited to the crude beginnings, the rudimentary development of human society: it does not include the maturer phases of that complex growth, still less does it embrace the practical problems with which our modern statesmen and law-givers are called upon to deal.

Thus Frazer conceived of social anthropology as the sociological study of "primitive" forms of society. Similarly, in his article on "Social Anthropology" in the 13th edition of the *Encyclopaedia Britannica* (1926), Malinowski defined the subject as "a branch of Sociology, as applied to primitive tribes." This adjective "primitive" must not be misunderstood. Frazer wrote:

Here it is necessary to guard against a common misapprehension. The savages of today are primitive only in a relative not an absolute sense. They are primitive by comparison with us; they are not primitive by comparison with truly primaeval man, that is, with man as he was when he emerged from the purely bestial stage of existence. Indeed, compared with man in his absolutely pristine state even the lowest savage today is doubtless a highly developed and cultured being, since all evidence and all probability are in favour of the view that every existing race of man, the rudest as well as the most civilised, has reached its present level of culture, whether it be high or low, only after a slow and painful progress upwards, which must have extended over many thousands, perhaps millions, of years. . . . While Social Anthropology has much to say of primitive man in the relative sense, it has nothing whatever to say of primitive man in the absolute sense, and that for the very simple reason that it knows nothing whatever about him, and, so far as we can see at present, is never likely to know anything.

It is, of course, not possible to draw any sharp dividing line between primitive and not primitive societies. Further, social anthropology can not and does not entirely confine its attention to the primitive societies. It is at least part of its task to compare primitive societies with those that are more advanced. In the past twenty years social anthropologists have carried out special studies of local communities in literate societies, in Ireland, Quebec, Massachusetts, Mississippi, Japan and China. The definitions of Frazer and Malinowski are no longer adequate to define social anthropology at the present day. We can say that it is characterised by a certain method of investigation, which can be applied either to primitive peoples or to communities of limited size in civilised societies, and that in pursuit of its theoretical aims social anthropology is obliged to pay special attention to the societies we call primitive.

It is necessary to say something about the distinction between social anthropology and ethnology, about which there is often some confusion of thought. It must be remembered, however, that the name "ethnology," like the name "sociology," is used differently in different countries and even in the same country by different writers or schools. Here we shall consider only the traditional meaning it has in England.

The name "ethnology" came into use a little more than a hundred years ago. As its etymology shows, it is the study of peoples (Greek *ethnos*). The Ethnological Society of London, founded in 1843, stated in its constitution that it was formed "for the purpose of inquiring into the distinguishing characteristics, physical and moral, of the varieties of Mankind, which inhabit or have inhabited the Earth." In the *Oxford Dictionary* ethnology is defined as "the science which treats of peoples and races, their relations, their distinctive characteristics, etc." The *Encyclopaedia Britannica* (14th edition) writes of ethnology and ethnography as "primarily sciences which deal with man as a racial unit, and with the distribution over the earth of racial units. They include a comparative study of the physical characteristics of the races of mankind and also a comparative study and classification of peoples based upon cultural conditions and characteristics."

The name "ethnography" is generally used for purely descriptive accounts of a people or peoples. Ethnology goes beyond description. In the first place it seeks to provide a classification of peoples by comparing them with reference to their similarities and differences. Peoples or ethnic groups resemble or differ from each other by racial characters, by language, and by their mode of life and mode of thought, from the kind of dwellings they inhabit or the kind of clothes they wear to the kind of beliefs they hold. Ethnologists distinguish between the racial characteristics of a people and their cultural characteristics and between racial and cultural classifications.

The distribution of peoples on the face of the Earth in recent times and their racial and cultural similarities and differences are the result of an exceedingly complex multitude of events which began when mankind first appeared, perhaps a million years ago; the process has been one of migrations, minglings, and interactions of peoples, of modifications of racial characters and of cultural changes and developments. For some peoples and for a few centuries some knowledge of the process is revealed to us by history, using that term in its common meaning as the authentic record—the story—of events and conditions of the past. Ethnologists concentrate a good deal of their attention on attempting to discover something about the prehistoric past.

One important source of knowledge is prehistoric archaeology, which may be regarded as a branch of ethnology. The archaeologist seeks the material remains of vanished peoples, finding the things they made and used and sometimes sufficient of their skeletal remains to determine some of their racial characters, and on geological evidence is often able to determine the geological date of the remains. The painstaking researches of archaeologists have given us a great and constantly increasing store of knowledge about the prehistoric inhabitants of many parts of the world.

The ethnologist seeks to draw inferences about prehistoric events and conditions by a consideration of the distribution of peoples in recent or historic times and a study of their resemblances and differences, either racial or cultural. The inferences have to be based on what may be called "circumstantial" evidence. Such evidence is in some instances entirely conclusive; for example the very close relationship between the Malagasy language of Madagascar and the languages of the Malay Archipelago is unquestionable evidence of a prehistoric connection between these two regions. Similarly, if we did not know from history that Negro slaves had been taken from Africa to the American continent, the racial resemblance of the negro inhabitants of the New World to those of Africa would enable us to infer with some degree of probability that there had been some movement of peoples across the Atlantic. But the hypotheses of ethnologists are sometimes highly speculative; and since it is notoriously difficult to reach agreement about circumstantial evidence there is much divergence amongst ethnologists in their interpretations.

Thus the problems with which ethnology has to deal are in the first place problems of racial and cultural classification, and secondly problems about the events of the prehistoric past. Typical questions for ethnology are: Where did the Polynesian peoples come from; by what route or routes and at what period or periods of time did they occupy the islands they now inhabit? How, when and where did the ancestors of the American Indians enter the continent, how did they spread over it and how did they develop those racial, linguistic and cultural differences which they exhibited when Europeans first made contact with them? The problems of social anthropology are of quite a different kind.

The aim of the social anthropologist is to make use of knowledge about primitive societies to establish valid and significant generalisations about social phenomena. It is in this sense that the subject may be called a kind of sociology. But "sociology" is a highly ambiguous word; it is applied to many different kinds of writings about society; much of what is called sociology has little or no connection with social anthropology.

The name "sociology" was invented by Auguste Comte. He believed, as Saint-Simon had done before him, that it is possible to apply to the study of human society the same methods of investigation that have been applied with such success in the study of physical and biological phenomena. He called this not yet existing science at first social physics, then sociology. But Comte did not himself write scientific sociology; what he did write may be better called philosophy of history. The idea that there could be a natural science of human society had been entertained since the seventeenth century. The avowed aim of social anthropology has been to contribute to the formation of such a science.

What characterises the natural sciences is the use of the experimental method of reasoning. There is a common misconception which confuses the experimental method with experimentation in the sense of operations by which an event to be observed is brought about by the experimenter. But the Latin *experiri* means only "to put to the test." What the experimental method really is, is a method of investigation and reasoning in which general ideas are systematically tested by reference to carefully observed facts. As Claude Bernard says in his "Introduction à l'étude de la médecine expérimentale," "The experimental method, considered in itself, is nothing other than a *reasoning* in the aid of which we methodically submit our ideas to the test of facts. The reasoning is always the same, in the sciences which study living beings just as much as in those which are concerned with inanimate bodies. But, in each kind of science, the phenomena vary and present a complexity and difficulties of investigation of their own."

Theoretical interest in human society and its institutions is not new. Theories of society were formulated by the Philosophers of China and Greece before the Christian era. At the present time there is an abundant literature on the subjects of social philosophy, political philosophy, philosophy of history, philosophy of religion and philosophy of art. The method of reasoning in these subjects must be distinguished from the experimental method of reasoning of the natural sciences.

One important difference is that in what we may call the philosophical method of enquiry it is commonly the aim to arrive at judgments of value. Philosophers are generally concerned with what societies might be or ought to be; they seek to define the "good" society or they distinguish between inferior and superior in systems of morality, law, government, economics, religion or art. It is the function of philosophers to guide men's actions by the discussion of desirable ends. Experimental reasoning can never give us judgments of value; it can only tell us what and how things are, never what things are good and what are bad. It can instruct us as to the appropriate means to a desired end; it cannot tell us what ends are desirable. If it is judged desirable to wipe out a town and its inhabitants, the experimental method can supply us with an atomic bomb.

There is an important difference between the philosophical method and the experimental method in the way in which they arrive at a body of connected generalisations which constitute a theory. The philosophical method is the older. The experimental method, after some tentative beginnings in ancient Greece, only came fully into use at the end of the sixteenth century in such work as that of Galileo. It replaced the philosophical method first in mechanics, astronomy and physics, and later in chemistry and the biological sciences. The last attempt of any importance to use the philosophical method to explain the phenomena of nature was the "Philosophy of Nature" of Hegel, and it is interesting to compare the results at which he arrived with those reached by the experimental scientists. But the experimental method has not yet replaced the philosophical method in the creation of theories of society.

Both methods combine observation with reasoning; the difference between them lies in the way in which these are combined. This difference was described by Francis Bacon.

There are and can be but two ways of investigating and discovering truth. The one flies from sense and particulars to the most general axioms, and from these as first principles, and their undisputed truth, determines and discovers middle axioms; and this is the way that is in use. The other draws out the axioms from sense and particulars, by ascending uniformly and step by step, so that at last it reaches the most general; and this is the true way, but untried. Each way begins from sense and particulars, and rests in the most general propositions: but yet they differ vastly; since the one touches cursorily on experience and particulars, while the other becomes duly and regularly familiar with them; the one again, from the first beginning, lays down some abstract and useless generalities; the other rises, step by step, to those things which are more familiar to Nature (i.e. higher abstractions).[1]

[1] Francis Bacon, *Novum organum* (1620), trans. Andrew Johnson, 1859, Book I, Aphorisms XIX and XXII. The term "axioms" (*axiomata*) used by Bacon means literally "something thought worthy of retaining," that is, generalisations for which there appears to be evidence. They would now be spoken of as "laws."

If we are ever to attain to a scientific knowledge of human society it can only be by systematically examining and comparing a number of diverse forms of society. Such a comparative study we may call "comparative sociology." It is a kind of sociology in which some small beginnings have been made, and it is of this kind of sociology that social anthropology can be said to be a part. If and when this comparative sociology ever becomes an established subject, social anthropology will be incorporated into it.

In comparative sociology great value and importance attaches to the systematic study of the simpler forms of society of what we call the primitive peoples. For this there are many reasons; one is that they reveal to us forms of social life that are very different from our own. The still surviving primitive societies are being rapidly destroyed or changed by their subjection to the technically more advanced peoples. This is a reason why social anthropologists, in seeking to make a contribution to comparative sociology, devote their attention chiefly, though not exclusively, to the study of these primitive forms of society before it is too late. The time is short, and the workers are few.

The experimental method is a method, the only scientific method, of arriving at inductive generalisations. Experimental observation is observation guided by general concepts. The most important task of the experimental scientist is therefore the invention of general or abstract concepts which he will apply to the analysis of observed facts and thereby test their scientific value. Mere observation and description cannot give us scientific knowledge; yet there are some who think that the piling up of observations will some day lead to advance of science. Charles Darwin wrote "How odd it is that anyone should not see that all observation must be for or against some view, if it is to be of any service." Claude Bernard, again, wrote "The experimental method cannot give new and fruitful ideas to men who have none; it can serve only to guide the ideas of men who have them, to direct their ideas and develop them so as to get the best possible results. As only what has been sown in the ground will ever grow in it, so nothing will be developed by the experimental method except the ideas submitted to it. The method itself gives birth to nothing. Certain philosophers have made the mistake of according too much power to method along these lines." Finally may be quoted the statement of Whewell: "It is necessary, in order to obtain from facts any general truth, that we should apply to them that appropriate idea, by which permanent and definite relations are established among them."[2]

Thus the task of comparative sociology, as of any experimental science, is to create the appropriate analytic concepts in terms of which we make generalisations, which, when tested sufficiently by systematic observations of the phenomena, can be established as having some probability. The special field of social anthropology is the experimental study, in the sense defined above, of primitive societies.

[2] *Novum organon renovatum.* See p. 166.

Chapter II

PRECURSORS

From the sixteenth century the accounts given by voyagers and travellers of the customs of the peoples of America, Africa and Asia attracted the attention of educated men in Europe. The impression that was made was that of the great diversity of social usages and institutions in different societies. This was a theme taken up by the Spanish writer Messie, and it was probably his *Leçons diverses*, translated into French in 1552 by Claude Gruget, that suggested to Montaigne his essay "De la coutume." An early attempt to provide an explanation of the diversity of peoples was made by Jean Bodin (1530–96) in his book *Les six livres de la république* (1576) in which he suggested that differences between peoples, including differences in their form of government, might be due to differences in the regions they inhabit, particularly differences of climate. The idea influenced Montesquieu and many later writers and is still entertained by some geographers at the present day.

By the beginning of the seventeenth century there had developed an interest in ethnological speculations. Just as in the present century Elliot Smith and his disciples thought they could trace the influence of the ancient Egyptians over a large part of the Earth, so in earlier times it was the "lost tribes of Israel" whose supposed traces were found in Asia and America. Edward Brerewood, who had been professor of astronomy in Gresham College in London, published in 1614 *Enquiries Touching the Diversity of Languages and Religions through the*

Chief Parts of the World. In the thirteenth chapter, on the distribution of the Jews, he rejects the hypothesis that the "Tartars," which name referred at that time to the inhabitants of a large part of Asia, are descended from the ten tribes of Israel. He holds that the custom of circumcision is "no sure token of descent from the Israelites." On the other hand he surmises that "the inhabitants of America are the offspring of Tartars," that is, that America was peopled from northern regions of Asia.

While Ethnology had its origin in these speculations about the prehistoric migrations of peoples, the comparative method which later developed into social anthropology had its origin in the idea that the customs of a particular people might be made comprehensible by comparing them with similar customs elsewhere. In 1703 there appeared a work entitled *Conformité des coutumes des Indiens orientaux avec celles des Juifs et des autres peuples de l'antiquité,* translated into English in 1705. The author says that he has made it his business "to inquire only after that which the Indians have in common with other Ancient People, but more particularly the Jews," without entering upon the question whether the resemblances he discovers were the result of the Jews' penetrating into India "or whether God in giving a Law to his People did not prescribe to them many things which the other Nations observed before, as being good in themselves." In 1700 Natalis Alexander had published his *Conformité des cérémonies chinoises avec l'idolâtrie grecque et romaine.* A more important work was that of Lafitau in 1729, *Mœurs des sauvages amériquains comparées aux mœurs des premier temps.* His aim was to throw light on the customs of antiquity by comparing them with similar customs of the American Indians whom he had visited. The President de Brosses made an early contribution to the comparative study of religions when he published in 1760 his work *Du culte des dieux fétiches, ou parallèle de l'ancienne religion de l'Égypte avec la religion actuèlle de Nigritie*. His work gave currency to the word "fetichism" as the name for religions such as that of West Africa.

The method adopted in these works was to compare the customs of existing peoples with those of the peoples of ancient times, the Jews, the Egyptians or the Greeks and Romans. Jean-Nicolas Démeunier (1751–1814) attempted something different. He published in 1776 his *L'esprit des usages et des coutumes des différents peuples ou observations tirées des voyageurs et des historiens* (3 vols.; à Londres, et se trouve à Paris). In explaining the plan of his work he remarks that although many books have been written about mankind there has been no general comparison of the manners, usages, customs and laws of the different peoples into which mankind is divided. This omission he wishes to repair, and while writers on the usages of other peoples have been concerned only with their bizarre or ridiculous aspects, he proposes a new method by which we seek their spirit (*esprit*). Démeunier was one of the founders of social anthropology, though his work is now almost forgotten and hardly ever read.

In the writers of the seventeenth and eighteenth centuries it is easy to discover two different interests in savage societies, one of which leads ultimately to ethnology and the other to social anthropology. These two interests were recognised by Dr. William Robertson, Principal of the University of Edinburgh and Historiographer to His Majesty for Scotland, in his *History of America*, published in two volumes in 1777. Robertson regarded the ethnological question of the origin of the American Indians as being of much less importance than the utilisation of knowledge about them in a study of human progress.

When the people of Europe unexpectedly discovered a New World, removed at a vast distance from every part of the ancient continent which was then known, and filled with inhabitants whose appearance and manner differed remarkably from the rest of the human species, the question concerning their origin became naturally an object of curiosity and attention. The theories and speculations of ingenious men with respect to this subject, would fill many volumes; but are often so wild and chimerical, that I should offer an insult to the understanding of my readers, if I attempted either to enumerate or to refute them [I, 265].

The condition and character of the American natives, at the time when they became known to the Europeans, deserve more attentive consideration, than the enquiry concerning their origin. The latter is merely an object of curiosity, the former is one of the most important as well as instructive researches, which can occupy the philosopher or historian. In order to complete the history of the human mind, and attain to a perfect knowledge of its nature and operations, we must contemplate man in all those various situations wherein he had been placed. We must follow him in his progress through the different stages of society, as he gradually advances from the infant state of civil life towards its maturity and decline [I, 281].

Robertson here gives one of the earliest definitions of the study that later came to be called social anthropology, and distinguished from the investigation of the origins of peoples which we now call ethnology.

The great increase of knowledge about the inhabitants of various parts of the world created for thinking men a problem, that of explaining the great diversity in the forms of human society. The answer to this problem was found in the theory of human progress or evolution. The theory is that throughout the life of mankind on Earth there has been a development of knowledge and of social institutions which has proceeded unequally in different parts of the world, and that the savage and barbarian societies of Africa, America and Oceania therefore represent in their most general characters conditions similar (but not identical) to those through which the more civilised societies have passed. The idea was, of course, not entirely new.

Lucretius had stated the doctrine of the progressive advance of mankind in the arts, and Thucydides had suggested that barbarous nations give us some idea of what civilised nations have been. While the idea of human progress was occasionally expressed in the seventeenth century, for example by Grotius, Fontenelle and John Locke, it was not until the following century that any systematic developments of it were undertaken. An account of these is to be found in *The Idea of Progress* by J. B. Bury (1920).

By the acceptance of the idea of progress there came into existence amongst the thinkers of the eighteenth century the idea that the social institutions of mankind—language, law, religions, etc.—had a natural origin and a natural development, and that the study of the simpler societies described by travellers would provide a means for a better understanding of human nature and of human society. The seventeenth century had witnessed immense developments of knowledge about nature as the result of the application of the experimental method of reasoning. There was aroused the desire to apply the same method of investigation to human life. David Hume, in 1739, described his *Treatise of Human Nature* as "an attempt to introduce the experimental method of reasoning into moral subjects."

The history of modern social science may be said to begin with the work of Montesquieu. He had been powerfully influenced by the Cartesian philosophy and wished to extend the Cartesian idea of natural law to social facts. In his *Considerations sur les causes de la grandeur des Romains et de leur décadence* (1734) Montesquieu expounded, and sought to apply, the idea that in historical happenings, besides the particular occasions which are usually looked upon as causes, there are general causes. It is the task of the philosopher, or as we should now say, the scientist, to seek to discover these general causes.

In 1748 Montesquieu published his most important book *De l'esprit des lois*. He had set himself to study "the laws, the customs and the diverse usages of all the peoples of the Earth. It may be said that the subject is immense, since it embraces all the institutions that are accepted amongst men."[1] The book he produced after many years of reading and thought was concerned with laws and with the relation of the laws of a society to the other features of the social system. There are many different kinds or types of society, and laws are different in different types. "Mankind are influenced by various causes—by climate, religion, by the laws, by the various precepts of government, by precedent, morals, and customs, whence is formed a general spirit of nations (*esprit général*). . . ." The methodological hypothesis of Montesquieu is that the various features of the social life of a society are inter-related as parts of a whole or system, and it is as the first clear formulation of this hypothesis that *The Spirit of Laws* is of such great importance in the history of social science. We shall see later that this hypothesis is a guiding principle of modern social anthropology.

About three years after the appearance of Montesquieu's work Turgot formulated his theory of social progress in his *Plan de deux discours sur l'histoire universelle*. Throughout the life of mankind there has been progress intermingled with episodes of decadence. Our own ancestors and the predecessors of the ancient Greeks resembled the savages of America as they were when they were discovered. We see progress in the arts every day, and we see in some parts of the world civilised and enlightened peoples and in others peoples wandering in the forests. There has been inequality of progress in different portions of mankind. The savages who live by hunting have not advanced as far as the pastoral peoples or the tillers of the

[1] *The Spirit of Laws*, Nugent translation (New York, 1949), p. 293.

soil. An attentive study of the peoples of the world, past and present, will enable us to create a "Universal History" which will embrace the consideration of the successive progressive developments of the human species and the details of the causes which have contributed thereto, disclosing the influence of general and necessary causes and that of particular causes and the free actions of great men, and the relation of all that to the constitution of human nature itself.

Turgot, however, did not pursue the study of which, as a young man, he had drawn up a plan. His friend and disciple the Marquis de Condorcet (1743–94) wrote in 1793 his *Esquisse d'un tableau historique des progrès de l'esprit humain.* This sketch of the history of human progress had considerable influence in the nineteenth century.

In the last half of the eighteenth century there was a group of British writers, many of them influenced by Montesquieu, and all of them accepting the idea of progress, who sought to develop an inductive study of social institutions by utilising the then available knowledge about the "rude and barbarous nations" which are now referred to as "primitive." Adam Ferguson wrote an *Essay on the History of Civil Society* (1767) and dealt with the same subject in his *Principles of Moral and Political Science* (1792). John Millar, in his *Origin of the Distinction of Ranks* (1771) compares the social institutions of rank, authority and property in different stages of social evolution which he classifies as those of Hunters and Fishers, Pastoral, Agricultural and Commercial. Other works were those of Lord Monboddo, *Of the Origin and Progress of Language* (6 vols., 1773–92), Lord Kames, *Sketches of the History of Man* (1774), James Dunbar, *Essays on the History of Mankind in Rude and Uncultivated Ages* (1780).

Adam Smith (1723–90) in his lectures on moral philosophy unfolded a general theory of society. The second part of these lectures was published in 1759 as the *Theory of Moral Sentiments*. The fourth part was expanded into his *Enquiry into the Nature and Causes of the Wealth of Nations*, printed in 1776. The third part dealt with justice and his plan was to follow the suggestion of Montesquieu and endeavour "to trace the gradual progress of jurisprudence, both public and private, from the rudest to the most refined ages, and to point out the effects of those arts which contribute to subsistence, and to the accumulation of property, in producing correspondent improvements or alterations in law and government." The book he planned on this subject was never completed, but notes of the lectures he delivered in 1763, taken by a student, were published in 1896 by Edwin Cannan, under the title *Lectures on Justice, Police, Revenue and Arms*. Smith's *Philosophical Essays*, published posthumously in 1795, "appeared to be parts of a plan he once formed, for giving a connected history of the liberal sciences and elegant arts."

In his introduction to the *Philosophical Essays*, (1810) Dugald Stewart defines the aim that Adam Smith pursued in all his writings.

When, in such a period of society as that in which we live, we compare our intellectual acquirements, our opinions, manners and institutions, with those which prevail among rude tribes, it cannot fail to occur to us as an interesting question, by what gradual steps the transition has been made from the first simple efforts of uncultivated nature, to a state of things so wonderfully artificial and complicated. . . . When the origin of the different sciences and of the rudiments to their last and most refined improvements? When the astonishing fabric of the political union; the fundamental principles which are common to all governments; and the different forms which civilised society has assumed in different ages of the world? On most of these subjects very little information is to be expected from history; for long before that stage of society when men begin to think of recording their transactions, many of the most important steps of their progress have been made. A few isolated facts may perhaps be collected from the casual observations of travellers, who have viewed the arrangements of rude nations; but nothing, it is evident, can be obtained in this way, which approaches to a regular and connected detail of human improvement. In this want of direct evidence, we are under a necessity of applying the place of fact by conjecture; and when we are unable to ascertain how men have actually conducted themselves upon particular occasions, of considering in what manner they are likely to have proceeded, from the principles of their nature, and the circumstances of their external situation. In such enquiries, the detached facts which travels and voyages afford us, may frequently serve as landmarks to our speculations; and sometimes our conclusions *a priori*, may tend to confirm the credibility of facts, which, on a superficial view, appeared to be doubtful or incredible.

To this species of philosophical investigation, which has no appropriate name in our language, I shall take the liberty of giving the title of *Theoretical* or *Conjectural History;* an expression which coincides pretty nearly in its meaning with that of *Natural History*, as employed by Mr. Hume, (see his "Natural History of Religion") and with what some French writers call *Histoire Raisonée*.

Dugald Stewart goes on to say that it is only lately that subjects such as law and government

have been considered in this point of view; the greater part of politicians before the time of Montesquieu, having contented themselves with an historical statement of facts, and with a vague reference of laws to the wisdom of particular legislators, or to accidental circumstances, which it is impossible now to ascertain. Montesquieu, on the contrary, considered laws as originating chiefly from the circumstances of society; and attempted to account, from the changes in the condition of mankind, which take place in the different stages of their progress, for the corresponding alterations which their institutions undergo. It is thus, that in his occasional elucidations of the Roman jurisprudence, instead of bewildering himself among the erudition of scholiasts and of antiquaries, we frequently find him borrowing his lights from the most remote and unconnected quarters of the globe, and combining the casual observations of illiterate travellers and navigators, into a philosophical commentary on the history of law and of manners.

The eighteenth century had opened up a path which leads to the scientific investigations of social anthropology or comparative sociology. There was the recognition of a new understanding of human society that could be reached by the comparison of the diverse forms of social life and its institutions; there was the idea of progress, affording an explanation of that diversity; there was the contribution of Montesquieu that in the historical development of societies there are general causes distinct from the accidental events of particular occasions; there was the other contribution of Montesquieu that the various features of social life in a particular region at a particular period are inter-connected to form some sort of systematic unity; finally there was the idea of "conjectural history" which played an important part in the first developments of social anthropology.

Underlying all this was the idea that the phenomena of the social life of mankind could be studied by the same methods of investigation that had produced such a great improvement of knowledge when applied to physical and biological phenomena. The possibility and necessity of a positive, inductive, study of human society as a whole was the burden of the preaching of two nineteenth century writers, Saint-Simon and Comte. Neither of them really developed the science about which they wrote; Saint-Simon was one of the founders of socialism, and endeavoured to establish a new religion; his disciple, Comte, was a philosopher who also founded a new religion of positivism. Both of them, however, were important figures in the development of social science. It was Comte who invented the name "sociology" for the positive science of society which he hoped to see created.

Chapter III

THE FORMATION OF SOCIAL
ANTHROPOLOGY

It has been shown in a previous chapter that in the eighteenth century the interest in non-European peoples led to two different kinds of enquiry. One of these concerned the historical origins of such peoples as the inhabitants of North America, or the peoples of the Pacific Islands, or the Australian and Tasmanian aborigines. This developed in the course of the nineteenth century into what can best be referred to as ethnological studies. The other was a philosophical enquiry into human progress, and it was from this that social anthropology had its beginning.

Ethnology made its appearance as a recognised branch of learning about 1840, and it developed very greatly during the next hundred years. There was a steady and very great increase in ethnographical knowledge, provided at first by travellers, and later by the work of field ethnographers. What had been "cabinets of curiosities" in earlier times became ethnological museums, which became centres for ethnological studies. The nineteenth century saw the rise and rapid progress of prehistoric archaeology. The interest in racial differences amongst the peoples of the world, and the idea that it would be possible to reconstruct a racial history of mankind, led to developments in physical anthropology. The study of comparative philology showed how it is possible to discover historical relations between languages.

One task of ethnology is the classification of peoples by reference to their racial characters, their languages and their culture. A second and connected task is to obtain knowledge of the history of peoples, for which there are no written records, by inference drawn from various kinds of circumstantial evidence. It is a kind of historical study that uses methods different from those of the historian. Franz Boas, whose teaching had very great influence in the United States, regarded this kind of study as constituting anthropology. For him the primary task of anthropology is "the reconstruction of history." "The science of anthropology" he wrote "deals with the history of human society. It differs from history in the narrower sense of the term in that its enquiries are not confined to the periods for which written records are available and to people who had developed the art of writing." Boas held that a feature of a society "is intelligible only from its past," so that the only kind of explanation that can be looked for in anthropology is historical explanation, of the kind that is afforded by the history of the historians. Sociological explanation is excluded. The following passage shows the idea that Boas had of the study of "historical anthropology."

The object of our investigation is to find the processes by which certain stages of culture have developed. The customs and beliefs are not the ultimate objects of research. We desire to learn the reasons why such customs and beliefs exist—in other words, we wish to discover the history of their development. . . . A detailed study of customs in their bearing to the total culture of the tribe practising them, and in connection with an investigation of their geographical distribution among neighbouring tribes, affords us almost always a means of determining with considerable accuracy the historical causes that led to the formation of the customs in question and the psychological processes that were at work in their development.[1] Whether we call this kind of anthropology "ethnology" or "historical anthropology" it is something different from social anthropology.

[1] Franz Boas *et al.*, *General Anthropology* (1938), Introduction.

Social anthropology, as has been said, had its origin in the philosophical investigation of human progress, and in those uses of comparison in the eighteenth century that have been mentioned in an earlier chapter, as represented in the writings of Montesquieu, de Brosses, Lafitau, Démeunier and others. The recognition of the great diversity in the forms of social life, in institutions, customs and beliefs, was the starting point. Comparisons, between Indians of North America and the peoples of antiquity, between religious customs of ancient Egypt and modern West Africa, and comparisons of various non-literate peoples showed that beneath this diversity there could be discovered certain resemblances. The purpose of the comparative method was to reveal these similarities amongst different and scattered peoples. For Démeunier the comparison of usages of different peoples would enable us to discover what he called their "spirit" or what some might now call their meaning. It was thought by Lafitau and others that the customs of ancient times might be better understood in the light of the resemblances they show to customs of non-literate peoples of later times. This use of comparison has been continued to the present day. Students of ancient Greece throw light on the society of that time by means of comparisons with features of the social life of primitive peoples. Frazer's *Golden Bough*, one of the classics of social anthropology, began as an attempt to understand the custom by which in ancient times the priest of the temple at Nemi obtained his office by killing the previous occupant. The explanation was sought by examining similar customs elsewhere, and led to the comparative investigation of many different customs and beliefs amongst non-literate peoples as well as the peoples of antiquity.

The comparative method, or the use of parallels between the habits and beliefs of one people and another, which came into use in the eighteenth century, involved the principle stated by Bergier in 1767 that *partout les hommes se ressemblent*. This was called in the nineteenth century, pedantically and misleadingly, the principle of the "psychic unity" of mankind. The real principle is that since human beings as we know them are the same kind of creatures, when they are associated in social life they are likely in different regions, and independently, to create similar forms of association with similarities in their institutions.

If we want a date we can put 1870 as being that of the beginning of social anthropology. One of the tasks of the new study was to explore the similarities of social features in different regions by the study of ethnographical and historical sources. Tylor collected and compared the varying beliefs about the human soul and its survival after death. McLennan drew attention to the existence in different regions of a custom by which each of a number of groups (clans) into which the society was divided had a special association with a particular species of animal or plant, which association was expressed in ritual or in myth. To this class of customs McLennan gave the name "totemism." Frazer, at the request of Robertson Smith, collected the available information about this for an article in the *Encyclopaedia Britannica*, which was later published as a book in 1887 and expanded in 1910 into the four volumes of *Totemism and Exogamy*. Morgan collected the systems of nomenclature used for relationships by kinship and marriage from all over the world, and revealed the very widespread resemblances in separate regions of what he called "classificatory systems." Frazer, again at the suggestion of Robertson Smith, and for the *Encyclopaedia Britannica*, collected the data about the customs known as "taboo." His *Golden Bough* in its final enlarged form is a corpus of customs and beliefs gathered from all over the world. He began at a later time the collection of data about the belief in immortality, on which, however, he only completed two volumes.

This exploratory survey of customs and beliefs to exhibit their diversity and underlying resemblances constituted the chief contribution of the early social anthropologists to the formation of the subject as an orderly discipline. One thing that was brought out by this labour of collection was that, in spite of the great diversity of primitive societies, there were certain features of custom and belief that were found widely distributed in societies between which there was no evidence for any past connection or communication. The resemblances could not, therefore, plausibly be explained as due to what ethnologists call "borrowing" or "diffusion," but call for some other kind of interpretation. The problem placed before the social anthropologists was, therefore, how to reduce the differences and resemblances of social customs and beliefs to some sort of order.

The guiding idea that they had received from the preceding century was that of progress, and the study of progress thus became a principal task of the study. It was recognised, as had been pointed out by Comte, that to make a study of progress we must take mankind as a whole. At different periods different regions make contributions to the general development of human knowledge or human life. It was the Semitic region, for example, that provided the alphabetic form of writing which is now so widely used.

The progressive development of mankind can most readily be seen in material techniques. General Pitt-Rivers was interested in the development from the simplest forms of weapons to the most advanced. The collection, extended to include many other kinds of technical productions, was presented to Oxford University as a museum of comparative technology to illustrate technical progress of mankind, being thus quite different from an ethnological museum which illustrates the ways of life of different peoples of the world. The study of techniques can in some instances show something of the order of development. The composite bow is an improvement on the simple bow; the cross-bow was derived from the ordinary bow. Successive steps in technical advance could thus be exhibited.

It was supposed in the last century that successive steps or stages of Comte had produced a theory of progress in human thought, the theory of the three stages. The first stage was that of religion, itself divided into three, represented by the religions of savages that Comte referred to as fetichism, succeeded by polytheism, which was in turn succeeded by monotheism; the second stage was that of metaphysics; the third and final stage was to be that of positivism, in which thought would be controlled neither by religion nor metaphysics but by positive science.

The hope of discovering successive stages of development in social institutions resulted in speculative hypotheses which became serious obstacles in the way of the development of a scientific social anthropology. A good example is provided by what was called the matriarchal theory. It was found that in some societies descent and succession, and inheritance of property, might go through the female line, so that a man would belong to the group of his mother's brother or might inherit his mother's brother's property or social position. The hypothesis was that these conditions represented survivals of an early condition of society of the existence of which there is no evidence whatever, in which kinship was reckoned only through females and the relation of father and child was not recognised. This hypothesis, independently formulated by Bachofen and McLennan, and unfortunately widely accepted, by Tylor, Frazer, Morgan, Durkheim and many others, greatly obstructed the study of kinship until the beginning of this century, and even later continued to exercise a pernicious influence not only on theorising but on observation.

The outstanding example of this attempt by anthropologists to establish by *a priori* reasoning an order of succession of social institutions or forms of society is provided by the *Ancient Society* of the American Lewis Morgan, published in 1877. Making use of his extensive ethnographical knowledge, he attempted to formulate a scheme of successive stages of human development which he thought to be represented by existing peoples. His theories were thoroughly unscientific and unhistorical, but had a romantic appeal, and, as presented by Engels, are now an essential part of orthodox Marxism.

These theories of successive stages in human development are frequently referred to as "evolutionary anthropology." They are really based on the conception of progress. Morgan, for example, thought of the history of mankind as a process of steady material and moral improvement. Such theories are in direct conflict with the idea of social evolution, for an essential feature of evolution is that it is a process of divergent development. All the recently existing forms of society represent the end result of such divergent development, just as insects, birds and mammals represent the end results of the divergent developments of organic evolution. Progress, on the other hand, as a process of improvement, is conceived as unilinear, as being the step by step improvement of the conditions of social life.

Early social anthropology inherited from the eighteenth century the idea of "conjectural history," the idea that the origin and development of some feature of social life may be discovered by *a priori* reasoning from "known principles of human nature." The assumption is that since we know how human beings behave and think, we can form a reasonable idea of how they came to originate some belief or custom or social institution. In early anthropology, therefore, the origin of various features of social life was a constant subject of speculation. There were various theories as to the origin of religion. Tylor offered a theory as to the origin of the belief in a soul surviving bodily death. Perhaps the best example of this kind of thing is afforded by totemism, the origin of which became a favourite subject of speculation and discussion. Van Gennep, in a review of the subject in 1920, was able to enumerate thirty-nine theories of the origin of totemism that had been put forward from 1870 to that date. Every writer on the subject produced his own hypothesis. There was an abundance of hypotheses, and a complete lack of agreement.

At the end of the nineteenth century it began to be felt by some students of the subject that these speculations as to the origin of features of social life, or as to the order of development of institutions, so far from advancing the science, were obstacles in the way of advance. If social anthropology was to be an experimental science it must admit only experimental hypotheses, and refuse consideration of any others. An experimental hypothesis is one that can be tested by reference to observations. It is impossible to test hypotheses as to origins, or as to succession in social institutions, either by historical records or by observation of existing societies. They have therefore no place in an experimental study.

There is an ambiguity in the idea of "origin." It may be taken to mean the particular conditions and events by which some feature of social life, such as totemism, came into existence in a particular region at a particular time, its *historical* origin. Or there may be an idea of a repeated causal process, so that, for example, the same kind of causal process would have given rise to totemism in different times and regions. Historical origins are only to be discovered by historical investigations. A hypothesis as to causal origin can only be supported by the actual observation of at least one instance of the process. The theories of origin of the last century did not afford either historical or scientific knowledge.

The theories of the origin of some category of customs most usually rested on an undeclared assumption as to the nature of the customs in question. Tylor's theory of the origin of religion was based on his view of religion as consisting of beliefs arrived at by erroneous processes of reasoning. Theories of the origin of totemism were based on assumptions as to the nature of totemic beliefs and practices. In place of the last-century speculations about origins, the anthropologists of this century are concerned with the problems of determining the nature of the institutions, customs and beliefs found in primitive societies. Important contributions to social anthropology were made by historians such as Fustel de Coulanges, Henry Maine and Robertson Smith. The last named writer is particularly important as the pioneer in the sociological study of religion in his work on early Semitic religion.

At the end of the nineteenth century English social anthropology was powerfully influenced by the work of Émile Durkheim and the writers who collaborated with him in the *Année sociologique*. Durkheim had been influenced not only by Montesquieu and Comte but also by English writers, Herbert Spencer, Robertson Smith, Frazer, and others. It was the aim of his life and work to lay firm foundations for a science of comparative sociology, and he recognised the immense importance for such a science of the systematic study of the forms of social life of primitive or non-literate peoples.

The French sociologists criticised the methods and the theories of the English social anthropologists. One of their criticisms was that in concentrating their attention on questions of origin they neglected any study of the social function of the institutions, customs and beliefs with which they were dealing. Two customs which seem to be similar may have different functions in the societies in which they exist, and are then not properly comparable. The function can only be discovered by examining the place that the custom has in the social system of which it is part.

A second criticism was that many of the theories of the anthropologists were psychological rather than sociological and based on an intellectualist psychology. The French sociologists argued that social phenomena need sociological explanation; that religion, for example, to be understood, has to be studied as specifically a social phenomenon. In this Robertson Smith had already led the way and Durkheim acknowledged the influence of this writer on his work. A particular religion has to be examined as a part of the social system of a society in which it exists, and cannot be explained by theories of psychology. This is simply a further application of the idea of Montesquieu about law. Thus totemism in Australia, or ancestor worship in an African tribe have to be examined in their social function, the part they play in a society organised in a certain way.

Another important influence was that of A. C. Haddon of Cambridge. He criticised the comparative method as used by Frazer and others, and urged that comparative studies ought to be based on what he called "intensive studies of particular societies." Haddon began his career as a zoologist, and he well knew that comparative morphology and physiology have to be based on careful anatomical and physiological studies of particular species. He held that a good part of the data used by the social anthropologists was of doubtful value or reliability, since it was derived not from accounts by trained scientific observers, but from missionaries and travellers who had had no training in the observation of social facts.

Further, he held that to understand any custom or belief in a primitive society, it is not sufficient to compare it with similar occurrences elsewhere, but it is necessary also to study it in its relation to the particular system of customs and beliefs of which it is a part. What was needed, therefore, was field research carried out by adequately trained investigators whose task it would be not simply to record the features of the social life but also to interpret them by an analysis of their interrelations. The Cambridge Expedition to Torres Straits in 1898 marked the beginning of a new phase in the development of social anthropology. Unfortunately, Haddon had the idea that the proper person to interpret social customs and beliefs would be a psychologist who accompanied the expedition; that section of the report was never published, or for that matter written. But Haddon's ideas were carried out by field workers in the twentieth century.

In the nineteenth century the theoretical work in social anthropology was separated from the work of observation. The theoretical anthropologist did not himself undertake the observation of primitive societies, but gathered his facts from the writings of others. No experimental science can be satisfactorily established on this basis; for in the experimental method reasoning or analysis and observation are intimately combined in a continuous process of investigation. The theoretical anthropologist who has not lived for a time in close contact with a primitive people is at a serious disadvantage in trying to make use of the material supplied by others. It is therefore now recognised that an essential part of the training of a social anthropologist is to carry out at least one piece of field research. On the other side, the field worker has to be equipped with a knowledge of the theories and hypotheses of the subject. It is his task to test existing hypotheses on the basis of his observations, which in their turn can be tested by comparative studies and by other observations on other societies.

Social anthropology is essentially the comparison of different forms of social life, of primitive societies one with another, with ancient societies about which we have historical knowledge, and with the advanced societies of the present. But comparison can be used in different ways and for different purposes. There is the scientific use of comparison, illustrated in the comparative morphology and physiology of animal species. The purpose of comparison in such studies is to arrive at classifications and generalisations; this may be called the "systematic" use. But comparisons may be used for the entirely different purpose of formulating a historical or genetic hypothesis.

The two different comparative methods are conveniently illustrated by reference to the study of language. The nineteenth century saw the growth of historical linguistics. By comparing languages it is possible to show that some of them are "genetically" related. The Teutonic languages (English, Dutch, German, Norwegian, etc.) can be demonstrated to have had a common origin at some time in the past, and linguists have been able to show that most of the languages of Europe and many of those of India have a common origin. Languages are classified "genetically" into "families" and "branches" of families, the Teutonic languages being one branch of the Indo-European family. From about 1880 a different kind of study of language came into existence, general linguistics, which is now an established branch of learning. In this study comparison of languages with one another is used, not for the purpose of discovering historical or genetic relations between them, but in order to discover and formulate the general characteristics of language as a special kind of social phenomena. In place of a genetic classification it aims at a classification by morphological types.

It is no part of the work of the social anthropologist to "reconstruct" history; he can leave that to the ethnologists, archaeologists and "historical anthropologists." The use of comparison by the social anthropologist is similar to its use in general linguistics or in comparative zoology. The purpose is to arrive at valid generalisations about the nature of society and social phenomena by the systematic study of resemblances and differences. By the use of abstractive generalisation, the more general, essential and permanent characteristics of social life are distinguished from the accidental and variable.

It has been thought by some that the reason for the study of these societies of savages is that it can reveal the social conditions of our own ancestors in ancient times. The proper understanding of the theory of evolution puts an end to this idea. The Australian aborigines do not represent a race from which we are descended, but a specialised race resulting from the racial divergence that has taken place in the species of Homo sapiens. The Australian form of society is similarly a specialised form that has resulted from the divergent development that is an essential feature of social evolution. It is as a specialised, not as an ancestral, form that the society of the Australian aborigines is of value for comparative study. If we wish to arrive at scientific knowledge of the nature of human society we can only do so by the systematic comparison of diverse types of society, and the more diverse they are the better. Just as the study of the lower forms of organic life is essential in biology, so the study of the lower forms of society (in the evolutionary sense) is essential to a science of sociology.

Chapter IV

SOCIAL STRUCTURE

Whewell, in his *Novum organon renovatum*,[1] describes inductive science as "the application of clear and appropriate ideas to a body of facts," and as requiring a double process of "explication of concepts" and "colligation of facts." Each science must advance by means of its *appropriate* concepts, and this requires the creation of a coherent system of technical terms. "In an advanced science, the history of the language of the science is the history of the science itself. . . . The fundamental principle and supreme rule of all scientific terminology is that terms must be constructed and appropriated so as to be fitted to enunciate simply and clearly true general proposition." Social anthropology is not yet an advanced science; it does not yet have a coherent system of concepts denoted by technical terms accepted and used in the same sense by all the students of the subject. This is the result, and at the same time the sign, of the immaturity of the science. One of the difficulties that the reader of the literature of anthropology has to face is the fact that the same word is used in different meanings by different writers, and many anthropological terms are sometimes used ambiguously or without precise definition.

In order to avoid confused and unscientific thinking it is necessary to obtain and keep constantly in mind a clear idea of the nature of the empirical reality with which we have to deal in social anthropology, and to which all our concepts and theories must be referred. Only in this way

[1] 3d ed., 1858.

can we hope to avoid the fallacy of "misplaced concreteness" which results from treating abstractions as though they were concrete realities, a fallacy which it is difficult to avoid. There is a tendency to think of "societies" as if they were separate discrete entities. This is derived from Aristotle, for whom a society was a *koinonia politike*, a political association such as the Greek city state. The collection of persons living in a defined area under a single political authority is only one kind of association. We might ask "Is the British Empire a 'society,' or, if not, how many distinct societies does it contain?" The Roman Church as a religious or ecclesiastical association is as much a society as a political association such as the United States. It is necessary to avoid the tendency to think of societies as discrete entities in the way in which Herbert Spencer did.

The empirical reality with which social anthropology has to deal, by description, by analysis and in comparative studies, is the process of social life of a certain limited region during a certain period of time. The social life as a phenomenal reality is a process consisting of a multitude of actions of human beings, more particularly their interactions and joint actions. The particular events of the social life are the facts to which all our concepts and theories must be applied. To provide a description of social life we have to describe certain *general* features which seem significant or relevant to our enquiries, and it is these generalised descriptions that provide the *data* of the science. It is obvious that importance attaches to the way in which these data are extracted, from direct observation or particular facts, from statements by informants, or from historical records.

Over a limited period the general features of the social life of a particular region may remain unchanged, or may change in only minor respects. In other instances, particularly if a sufficient period be taken, there will be significant changes in some features. We can distinguish between a *synchronic* description in which the social life is taken as it is at a certain time without reference to changes in its general features, and a *diachronic* description which gives an account of such changes.

Two very important concepts are *social structure* and *social organisation*. The concept of structure refers to an arrangement of parts or components related to one another in some sort of larger unity. We can talk of the structure of a house, meaning the arrangement of walls, roof, rooms, stairs, passages, etc., and ultimately as an arrangement of bricks, stone, timber, etc. We can speak of the structure of a piece of music as an arrangement of successive sounds, and we can say that the structure of one fugue or sonata is similar in *form* to that of another. The structure of a molecule is the arrangement of its component atoms in relation to one another. The structure of a human body is in the first instance an arrangement of tissues and organs, but ultimately an arrangement of living and dead cells and interstitial fluids.

In social structure the ultimate components are individual human beings thought of as actors in the social life, that is, as *persons*, and structure consists of the arrangement of persons in relation to each other. The inhabitants of Europe are arranged into nations, and this is therefore a structural feature of the social life of Europe. In a village we may find an arrangement of persons into families or households, which is again a structural feature. In a family the structure consists of the relations of father, mother and children to each other.

Thus in looking for the structural features of social life we look first for the existence of social groups of all kinds, and examine also the internal structure of those groups that we find. But besides the arrangement of persons into groups and within those groups we find also an arrangement into social classes and categories. Social distinctions between men and women, between chiefs or nobles and commoners, between patricians and plebians, between Brahmins, Sudras and untouchables, are important structural features, though we cannot properly speak of these as forming social groups. Further, a most important structural feature is the arrangement of persons in dyadic, person to person, relationships, such as that between master and servant, or, in primitive societies between mother's brother and sister's son. Ultimately, a social structure is exhibited either in interactions between groups, as when one nation goes to war with another, or in interactions between persons.

While structure refers to arrangements of persons, organisation refers to the arrangement of activities. A gardener or peasant may be said to organise his own work when he allots different tasks to different seasons of the year. Social organisation is the arrangement of activities of two or more persons which are adjusted to give a united combined activity. An example is the organisation of work in a factory, whereby the manager, the foremen, the workmen, each have certain tasks to perform as part of the total activity. An organised group, which may consist of only two persons, is one in which the members combine in a joint activity in which each has an allotted part. We cannot, however, regard such groups as features of the social structure unless they have some degree of permanence. A football team is an organised group, but not the assembly of people who help to pull an overturned motor car out of a ditch.

These concepts of structure and organisation can be illustrated by reference to a modern army. The structure consists in the first place of the arrangement into groups—divisions, army corps, regiments, companies, and so on; and secondly of the arrangement of the personnel into ranks—generals, colonels, majors, corporals, "other ranks," etc. A rank is not a group; the majors, for example, do not constitute a social group but form a social category, like plumbers, bookmakers or University Professors. But the arrangement into ranks is an essential feature of the structure of an army. The organisation of the army is the allotment of activities of various kinds to the groups and individuals, whether in time of peace, or in actual military operations. A modern army is the best example of a highly organised structure; a Socialist State would have to be something similar.

The best way to make clear the concept of social structure is by an example, and we may take for this purpose the structural system of the tribes of a part of Western Australia as it was in former times. The essential basis of the structure was provided by the division of the country into a number of recognised distinct territories. Every male was attached by birth and throughout his life to one of these, that of his father and his father's father. The men thus connected with a particular territory formed a distinct social group which we speak of as a "clan," and this was a unit of fundamental importance in the social structure. A woman also belonged to the clan of her father, but since marriage between persons of one clan was forbidden, the women married men from other clans and became attached to the territory of the husband.

The men of a clan, together with their wives, coming from other clans, and their children, formed a group that it is convenient to call a *horde*, which may be described as occupying the territory of the clan. The horde camped together as a unit whether in their own country or when they were visiting friendly territories. A horde may be described as being politically autonomous, under the authority of the old men, and as being very largely self-sufficient economically. It probably numbered, on the average, not more than fifty persons.

The internal structure of the horde was a division into

families, each composed of a man with his wife or wives and their young children. It was a domestic group under the man's authority, having its own family hearth and shelter and its own food-supply. The family as a group was formed by marriage and the birth of children and came to an end as a separate group on the death of the husband, thus having continuous existence for only a limited number of years. The clan was a continuing group which the natives themselves thought of as having come into existence at the beginning of the world, and as being eternal; as members were lost by death they were replaced by the birth of new members. The continuity of the horde as a group of persons living regularly together was somewhat different. The male members of the clan constituted the continuing nucleus of the horde, but the female members moved out when they married, and other women moved in as wives of the men.

There were wider systems of structure. A number of clans had the same language, and had similar customs; they therefore formed a linguistic community, which is referred to as a *tribe*. Unlike what are called tribes in some other regions, this was not a politically united group; the members of a tribe did not unite in any combined action. Hordes of the same tribe or of different tribes might live at peace with one another, or might on occasion engage in fighting.

Persons of different hordes and of different tribes were linked together by means of the kinship system. A man was connected by some relation of kinship, near or distant, with every person with whom he had any social contact, no matter to what horde or tribe they belonged. The basis of the reckoning consisted of actual genealogical relationships, including therein the relations between fellow-members of one clan. The kin of any given person were classified into a limited number of categories, each denoted by one kinship term, but distinguished within the category as being nearer or more distant. The behaviour of any two persons towards one another was dependent on the relationship in which they stood in the kinship structure. The structure was a complex arrangement of dyadic, person to person, relationships. A particular man was closely connected through his mother with her clan and its members. He could always visit their territory and live with the horde though he was not and could not become a member of the clan. Different members of a single clan were connected in this way with different other clans. The same thing results from the fact that a man was connected with the clan of his mother's mother, and with the clan from which he obtained a wife. Each person had his own particular position in the total kinship structure. Even two full brothers might marry into different clans, although they had the same connection with their mother's clan.

There is a division of the society into two moieties, and this division extends through a number of tribes. Each clan belongs to one of the moieties. We may denote the moieties as I and II. Essentially the system is a classification or grouping of clans, which cuts across the classification into tribes or linguistic communities. A man distinguishes the clans with which he is acquainted as belonging to the same moiety as his own or to the other moiety. There is a further dichotomy of society into two alternating generation divisions, which can be denoted as x and y. If a man belongs to the x division his children will be y, and so will his father, while his father's father and his son's son will be x like himself. Each clan therefore contains at all times persons of both divisions. There is therefore a four-fold division of society, into what it is convenient to call "sections," the four being Ix, Iy, IIx and IIy. These sections have names—such as Banaka, Burong, Karimera and Paldjeri. By the laws of these tribes a man may only marry a woman who belongs to one of the categories into which his kin are arranged, that which includes the daughter of his mother's brother. The result is that he must find a wife in his own generation division and in the opposite moiety from his own; a man of Ix has to find a wife in IIx; in the Kariera tribe a man of Banaka section had to find a wife in the Burung section. If by "social group" we mean a body of persons having a certain cohesion, the clans and hordes are groups in this sense, but the sections are not. They provide a kind of classification of persons within the intertribal kinship structure, and are part of that structure.

There are other aspects of social structure that should be mentioned. Each clan is a distinct totemic group, having its own sacred totem-centres within its territory, its own myths of the origin of the topographical features of the territory and of these sacred spots, and its own rites which are carried out with the ostensible purpose of maintaining the continuity of nature and of society. Each clan has its own totemic solidarity and continuity, which differentiates it from other clans. But, in addition, there are totemic ceremonies and religious rites for the initiation of boys in which a number of clans unite and co-operate. Meetings of clans in the territory of one of them are held at intervals; on different occasions it is a different collection of clans that assembles, since a meeting held in the territory of a particular clan will only be attended by neighbouring friendly clans. It is the clans and their meetings that provide the religious structure of society.

Each of these meetings can be regarded as creating a temporary political group, for at them conflicts between clans or between individual members of different clans are settled under the authority of the assembled public opinion. This is the nearest approach that these tribes have to a political organisation wider than the horde.

In these tribes, as elsewhere in Australia, there was a continuous circulation of certain kinds of articles by exchanges of gifts, whereby they passed from one horde to another. These exchanges were less important economically than as maintaining relations of friendship.

In many societies an important element of the structural system is the division into social classes, such as the division between chiefs and commoners in Polynesia. In Australian tribes there are no distinctions of this kind except on the basis of sex and age, but this is of very great importance. Men and women have different occupations. Authority is exercised in all social affairs by the older men, who are also the ritual leaders.

This description of a structural system in a primitive people may help to make clear certain matters. To arrive at a description of a structural system we have not only to consider social groups, such as the family, the clan and the horde, in Western Australia, with the internal structure of the group and the relations between the groups, and also social classes, but we have to examine the whole set of socially fixed relationships of person to person, as in the Australian kinship system. The social reality of groups and classes consists in the way in which they affect the interactions of persons, as belonging to the same or different groups or classes. From this point of view the structure of a region at a particular time consists of the whole set of social relationships in which the persons of that region are involved.

In any of the relationships of which the social structure consists there is an expectation that a person will conform to certain rules or patterns of behaviour. The term *institution* is used to refer to this, an institution being an established or socially recognised system of norms or patterns of conduct referring to some aspect of social life. The family institutions of a society are the patterns of behaviour to which the members of the family are expected to conform in their conduct in relation to one another. There are patterns or norms of conduct for a father towards his children, for a wife to a husband and vice versa, for child to parent, for brother to brother or sister. These institutions are accepted in a particular society, of which they are the institutions, as fixing, with a certain measure of flexibility, the *proper* conduct of a person in a certain relationship. They define for a person how he is expected to behave, and also how he may expect others to behave. Not every one always behaves as he ought, as he is expected to; minor or major deviations are frequent in any society; to deal with these there are *sanctions* of various kinds. Social structure therefore has to be described by the institutions which define the proper or expected conduct of persons in their various relationships. The structural features of social life of a particular region consist of all those continuing arrangements of persons in institutional relationships which are exhibited in the actions and interactions that in their totality make up the social life.

A question that needs to be mentioned, though it can only be dealt with very briefly, is that of structural continuity. We may first consider the continuity of social groups. A group such as a nation, a tribe, or a clan may have a continuous existence although its membership is continually changing, since it loses members by death and gains new members by birth. A learned society loses members by death or resignation but replaces them by electing new members. The French Academy continues to keep its identity although the members are now an entirely different set of persons from the members in the eighteenth century.

The same sort of continuity can be observed in social classes. In a Polynesian society the class of chiefs is continuous since when a chief dies he is replaced, in some instances by his eldest son. An occupational or professional class may have the same kind of continuity; as doctors or lawyers die or retire their places are taken by new recruits to the profession. A regiment in the army may have a continuous existence though there is a more or less continuous change of the persons who form it, and though lieutenants may become captains and then majors, and colonels, the arrangement of ranks remains the same. The United States always has a President, and England has a King, though the person who occupies this position in the social structure changes from time to time. The English House of Commons or the United States House of Representatives maintains its continuity in spite of changes in membership at each election.

Thus, as social structure is an arrangement of persons in institutionalised roles and relationships, structural continuity is the continuity of such arrangements. This may be conveniently expressed by means of the ideas of matter and form. In the static continuity of a building both the matter, the bricks, timber, tiles, etc., and the form remain the same. In a human body the matter consists of molecules, and this is constantly changing; my body does not consist of the same molecules as it did yesterday, and there is a popular idea that at the end of seven years every molecule of a human body has been replaced. But a human organism retains its form, excluding such changes as the amputation of a leg. The structural continuity of an organism is thus a dynamic, not a static, continuity, a process in which the matter of which the organism is composed is continually changing while the form remains the same. Structural continuity in human societies is dynamic in this sense, the matter being individual human beings, the form being the way in which they are connected by institutional relationships.

An aspect that has to be considered is the fact that individuals change their position in social structure during the course of life. A man may change his nationality, or leave one church to join another. What is everywhere present is the process by which a human being begins life as an infant and grows into an adult; the social position of a person changes, either gradually, or by institutionally defined stages, as from a boy he becomes a young man and finally an elder. In some African societies a very important structural feature is a system of age-grades, an individual passing from one grade to the next in accordance with the institutional pattern.

Social structure, therefore, is to be defined as the continuing arrangement of persons in relationships defined or controlled by institutions, i.e., socially established norms or patterns of behaviour.

Chapter V

SOCIAL EVOLUTION

The theory of social evolution was formulated by Herbert Spencer in 1860 in an essay on "The Social Organism" and developed in his *Principles of Sociology*, the publication of which was begun in 1876. The theory may be said to be the result of bringing together into what Spencer himself called a "synthetic philosophy" two ideas that had come down from the eighteenth century. One of these was the idea of transformism in organic life, or as it has been called since Spencer "organic evolution." The other was the idea of progress in human society.

During the second half of the eighteenth century the belief in the fixity of animal and plant species was undermined by the work of biological scientists, such as Adanson, de Maupertuis, Buffon, Erasmus Darwin, Cabanis and Lacépède. These scientists prepared the way for the theory of organic evolution, which was first definitely formulated by Lamarck in his inaugural address to a course on zoology on 21 Floréal of the year VIII of the Revolution (1800). There were evolutionists in biology, of whom Spencer was one, before Charles Darwin, but it was the publication of his *Origin of Species* (1859) that brought the theory into prominence. The theory of human progress had reached its culmination in the writers of the latter part of the eighteenth century, and had become an accepted idea of the nineteenth century. Spencer, who had been influenced by Comte, began his study of society in terms of progress, as may be seen in his *Social Statics*, published in 1851.

We do not need to consider Spencer's theory of the universe as an evolving universe, but may confine our attention to his theory of social evolution. Spencer held that the development of organic life and the development of the social life of mankind are instances of a single kind of process, for which he proposed the name "evolution." The idea of evolution is that of a progressive actualisation of potentialities, of organic life in the one and of social life in the other instance. The theory can be reduced to three essential propositions. (1) Both organic evolution and social evolution are natural processes subject to natural law. (2) The process of evolution is one of divergent development. All the various living and extinct species of animals and plants have been produced from a small number of early simple forms of living matter; the diversity in the forms of organic life is the result of the divergent development that is characteristic of evolution. Similarly, the various forms of social life existing at present, or known to us from history, have been produced by a process of divergent development. (3) In both organic and social evolution there has been a general trend, which Spencer calls the "advance of organisation." In organic evolution organisms of more complex structure and function have been developed by progressive steps from simpler ones, vertebrates from invertebrates, warm-blooded from cold-blooded animals, for example. In social evolution societies with more complex structure or organisation have been progressively developed from less complex forms. Evolution therefore, as it is conceived in theory, is both a process of diversification in the forms of organic or social life, and a process of "advance of organisation," organic or social. It is to be remembered that, as T. H. Huxley said, "evolution is not an explanation of the cosmic process, but merely a generalised statement of the method and results of that process."

Spencer's philosophy emphasises the unity and continuity of nature, and of evolution as a natural process. The evolution of mind, the development of more complex forms of mental activity out of simpler forms, is a feature of organic evolution. Social evolution, or what he also calls "super-organic" evolution, is, for Spencer, a continuation of the process of organic evolution. There can, he says, be no absolute separation between organic and super-organic evolution. "If there has been Evolution, that form of it here distinguished as super-organic must have arisen by insensible steps out of the organic. But we may conveniently mark it off as including all those processes and products which imply the co-ordinated actions of many individuals—co-ordinated actions which achieve results exceeding in extent and complexity those achievable by individual actions."

The development of social life amongst animals is an important feature of organic evolution. Amongst the lower forms of animal life biologists have studied what Allee calls the "mass physiology" of animal aggregations. The collecting together of animals of one species in the same neighbourhood is frequently beneficial to them; it may in some instances alter the environment, such as the water in which they swim, to make it better suited to their life. If we regard such aggregates as being not truly social, but following Allee, call them "sub-social," then, taking the whole field of animal life, we have to recognise that "there are no hard and fast lines that can be drawn between social and sub-social organisms." "All that can be found is a gradual development of social attributes, suggesting . . . a substratum of social tendencies that extends throughout the entire animal kingdom. From this substratum social life rises by the operation of different mechanisms and with various forms of expression until it reaches its present climax in vertebrates and insects."[1] At

[1] W. C. Allee, *The Social Life of Animals* (New York: W. W. Norton & Co., 1938), pp. 274–75.

a relatively early stage of animal evolution two lines diverged, one leading to the insects, the other to the vertebrates, and, by another divergence, to birds on the one side and mammals on the other. It is amongst the most highly evolved insects, birds and mammals that we find the most developed forms of social life.

For the evolutionist the human genus, including extinct species as well as the still surviving species of Homo sapiens, is the product of organic evolution, and the human mind is the product of the neuro-psychic development that is part of organic evolution. With respect to super-organic evolution there is a very important difference between human beings and other social animals. In the latter the form of social life is the same in all populations of one species, but in human life different aggregations of human beings have different forms of social life. Super-organic evolution in mankind is a process that is no longer dependent on organic evolution, that is, on developments in the inborn characteristics of the species. There is a wide gap in our knowledge of the whole evolutionary process, for we are, and must remain, entirely ignorant of the forms of social life of the earliest human beings or of their immediate pre-human ancestors. We know nothing about the social life of *Sinanthropus pekinensis*. It is reasonable to fix the real change from pre-human to human social life by reference to the beginnings of language.

The theory of social evolution, then, is not only that there has been divergent development in the forms of social life in different portions of mankind, but also that there has been "advance in organisation" which has not taken place evenly. There are certain misconceptions that must be avoided. Spencer wrote: "Evolution is commonly conceived to imply in everything an *intrinsic* tendency to become something higher; but this is an erroneous conception of it." A society which has reached a stage of internal and external equilibrium may continue without any important change of structure. "Change does not necessarily imply advance. Often it is towards neither a higher nor a lower structure. Only occasionally is the new combination of factors such as to cause a change constituting a step in social evolution. It is quite possible, and, I believe, highly probable, that retrogression has been as frequent as progression." The same thing is true of organic evolution. Julian Huxley writes: "Much of the minor systematic diversity to be observed in nature is irrelevant to the main course of evolution, a mere frill of variety superimposed upon its broad pattern."

An evolutionary process is essentially a combination of accident and law, and by reason of the element of accident it cannot be foretold. No biological knowledge, however extensive, could have foretold that from the original five-toed ancestor of the horses there would ultimately be derived the English race-horse and cart-horse of today; inversely, if we had not the paleontological evidence it would be impossible to know the kind of animal from which the modern horse has evolved.

Spencer emphasised as a factor of social evolution what he called "the increasing size of the social aggregate, accompanied, generally, by increasing density." The idea that in the course of social development small-scale associations, small in number of persons and in geographical area, are absorbed into or supplemented by large-scale ones, had been formulated before Spencer. Saint-Simon held that the most salient fact in history is the continual extension of the principle of association, as in the series family, city, nation, super-national church. Comte derived the idea from Saint-Simon, and preceded Spencer in expounding it. Durkheim, following Spencer, phrases the idea by saying that the dominant trend of social evolution has been "the progressive extension of the social milieu."

Spencer tended to think of societies as discrete entities, just as are organisms, and this will not do. It is therefore necessary to find some way of re-formulating Spencer's idea. If we place ourselves in some particular region at a certain period, for example in an Australian tribe, we can form an approximate idea of what may be called the sphere of interactions in which the persons we are observing are involved. Interaction in this sense includes hostile interactions as well as friendly ones; there is interaction in native Australia when one horde fights another. In the recent war there was interaction of a hostile kind between the United States and Japan. We can therefore reformulate the statements of Spencer and Durkheim by defining the factor of evolution to which they refer as being the progressive extension of the sphere of interaction.

The extent of a sphere of interaction is to be measured primarily not in terms of geography but by reference to the number of persons with whom those in a given region do or may interact. Thus an increase in the density of population of a region has the effect of increasing the size of the sphere of interaction. In this connection we may refer to Durkheim's distinction between material density and social density; the former is measured by the number of persons living in a unit area, such as a square mile; the latter is increased, irrespective of the material density, by increasing communications and increasing frequency of interactions.

Where interactions are frequent or continued they tend to take on standard form, and so to become to a greater or less extent institutionalised. The geographical extension of the sphere of interaction therefore makes possible, and often tends to produce, wider systems of social integration. For Spencer "integration" is "the primary trait of evolution," and it is as leading to wider and more complex forms of social integration that the "increase in size of the social aggregate," which is here called the increase in size of the sphere of interactions, is such an important factor of social evolution. There are different modes of social integration which can be combined in different ways in the same region. Spencer tended to think in terms of political, or combined political and economic, integration. This would leave out of account such a society as the Roman Church, and in the society of the Australian aborigines would omit the integration provided by the kinship system.

In a first attempt to compare societies with reference to the size of the sphere of interaction it is useful to consider language. In the most primitive societies of which we have knowledge, the primary group is a small group of persons attached to a certain territory. These groups are small in size, often including less than 100 men, women and children, and rarely, if ever, exceeding 200. A certain small number of such groups have a common language and thus form a linguistic community, and in such a community they usually observe the same customs and have a common system of ideas. This kind of social structure may be spoken of as that of the loose or decentralised tribe. The tribes or linguistic communities are small, numbering only a few hundred individuals, from about 200 as a minimum to perhaps 2,500 as a maximum for this type of structure, as it is found amongst "savages" who live by hunting, fishing and gathering natural products. It is true that in such primitive societies a person often learns to speak a language other than his or her own, and that where two neighbouring languages are similar in grammar and vocabulary communication is possible, or even fairly easy between persons of different tribes. Nevertheless, the small size of the linguistic community does give an indication of the limited size of the sphere of interaction. We can contrast such a condition with that of the present day in which English or Spanish or Arabic is spoken as their native language by millions of people.

The history of Latin illustrates the connection that sometimes exists between language and the processes by which spheres of interaction are expanded or contracted. Latin was originally the language of a small group of people in Latium. With the foundation of the city state of Rome and the military conquests that resulted in the formation and growth of the Roman Empire, Latin became the spoken language of a large part of Western Europe, displacing many other languages, Etruscan and a number of Italic and Celtic languages. The linguistic unification went along with the process of political integration by conquest, but for reasons that it is not difficult to discover Latin did not become the spoken language of the Eastern Empire. The process of expansion ceased after the second century, and with the decline of the Roman Empire there succeeded a process of political disintegration. The Latin language split into a large number of different spoken dialects. Latin as a written language was kept alive by the Roman Church, but it was only used by the educated classes. When the process of political reintegration began it led to the formation of a number of separate nations in what had been the Western Empire. From the many Latin dialects there came into existence the present Romance languages—French, Provençal, Italian, Catalonian, Castilian, Portuguese.

Spencer, thinking of societies as discrete entities, each consisting of the population of a limited and defined region, thought of increase in the size of the social aggregate as being the result of the incorporation of smaller societies into larger ones. He wrote that "the formation of a larger society results only by the combination of smaller societies; which occurs without obliterating the divisions previously caused by separation." But a society in Spencer's sense of the word can increase in what he calls "mass" by the growth of population, for "mass" refers to the number of individuals composing a group. Sociologists have recognised the increase of populations as one of the important factors of social evolution.

Why should mere size, here interpreted to mean the number of persons involved in the interactions that make up social life, be regarded as being in itself a factor in the growth of complexity of social structure? The answer lies in what is known to scientists as the "principle of similitude," which was expounded by Galileo three hundred years ago. Roughly stated, this is that for any kind of structure there are limits to its size; thus Nature cannot produce trees beyond a certain height on our Earth, and Galileo estimated the limit at about 300 feet. The recognition of this principle as applied to social structure is an essential item in the theory of social evolution. Simmel, for example, wrote that "every quantitative increase of a society results in qualitative modification, requires new adaptations. The forms of groups depend strictly on the number of the elements; a structure which is suitable for a social group of a certain membership loses its value if this increases."

Social evolution, as conceived by the creator of the theory, is essentially the development of the "structures and functions which make up the organisation and life of each society," from simpler to more complex forms. Spencer also recognised "certain associated developments which aid, and are aided by, social evolution, the developments of language, knowledge, morals, aesthetics." As one of the "factors" of social evolution he included "the accumulation of super-organic products which we commonly distinguish as artificial, but which, philosophically considered, are no less natural than all others resulting from evolution." Amongst these he included material appliances, language, the development of knowledge ending in science; the development of laws, mythologies, theologies; codes of propriety, good conduct, ceremony; and the complex group of "products we call aesthetic." All these developments are thought of, hypothetically, as being not entirely independent but connected with the development of social structure. What is the nature of the connections is, of course, a matter for investigation.

What is commonly thought of as "progress" is the accumulation of knowledge and the improvement of techniques through inventions and discoveries, leading from the conditions of savage tribes to the scientific and technical achievements of modern societies. For the theory of evolution, progress in this sense is both dependent on that development of organisation which is the essential feature of social evolution, and is also one of the factors on which the latter in turn depends. For example, the progress in knowledge and techniques in the more complex societies has depended on the increasing development of what is called "division of labour" but is more correctly described as increasing differentiation of occupations into a complex occupational structure, and this, in its turn, has been dependent on technical progress and accumulating knowledge.

Julian Huxley has written "Evolution may be regarded as the process by which the utilisation of the earth's resources by living matter is rendered progressively more efficient." Evolutionary advance is a matter of the development of forms of adaptation, and adaptation is both external and internal. Advance in external adaptation is what Huxley speaks of as "a raising of the upper limit of biological efficiency, this being defined as increased control over and independence of the environment." Advance in internal adaptation he speaks of as "a raising of the upper level of all-round functional efficiency and of harmony of internal adjustments." In the evolution of human societies advance in external adaptation has been attained, not by modifications of human organism, but by what has above been called progress. It is advance in the adjustment of human beings to the physical environment in which they live. Advance in internal adaptation has been attained by the adjustment of human individuals in systems of orderly relations. This we might very well speak of as "social coaptation." It is what is properly meant by civilisation if we consider the derivation of that word; for *cives* were the persons who lived together in an institutionally ordered community, as distinguished from *hostes*, from whom one could only expect inimical action. In organic evolution external and internal development are interdependent. In social evolution there is a measure of interdependence between the adaptation of a group to its environment and the "functional efficiency and harmony of internal adjustments" which constitute social coaptation.

We may divide the social evolution of the *Hominidae* into three phases. Of the first we know and can know nothing; this was the phase of the first development of the use of tools, of language, of morals, and presumably of religion, or at least of belief in supernatural forces. For the second phase we know with certainty nothing of the actual happenings, and the conjectures of ethnologists and conclusions of archaeologists do not give us much help. What we can observe are the products of this phase, the various forms of social life of the non-historic peoples. The third phase is that about which we have historical knowledge, which covers for a limited period of not more than six thousand years a limited part of the surface of the Earth. This third phase is the field of historical studies. There need be, however, no self-denying ordinance which would prevent social anthropologists' having a good deal to say about the conditions and events of this phase. Still, the major occupation of social anthropologists is with those forms of social life that represent, surviving into modern times, the second phase of evolution before men had invented the art of writing and could leave written records, however imperfect, of themselves and their lives. What has to be remembered is that no non-historic society represents the form from which any historic society is derived. No surviving reptile can be regarded as the ancestral form from which birds or mammals were evolved.

This book is written from the point of view of one who has all his life accepted the hypothesis of social evolution as formulated by Spencer as a useful working hypothesis in the study of human society. But the reader should be warned that in anthropology there is a very strong anti-evolutionist movement, the leader of which was Franz Boas at the beginning of this century. In 1918 a distinguished American ethnologist (Laufer) could write that to his mind the theory of social evolution is "the most inane, sterile and pernicious theory ever conceived in the history of science." It has not been considered necessary to include in this book any discussion of the views of the anti-evolutionists. Their writings show an amazing confusion of thought and ignorance of the theory of social evolution. The movement was an attempt to divert anthropologists from social anthropology as a sociological study of primitive societies to historical anthropology as a reconstruction of history; in the United States it was for a long time successful.

Social Anthropology

The late A. R. Radcliffe-Brown's writings stand today as import
definitions of the scope and method of the field of social anthropolo

"The collection contains some of the classic writings of Radcliffe-Brow
extending as far back as 1923, and from these the student and the gen
reader can ascertain some of the qualities which made him so influentia
the development of modern anthropology."—*Pacific Affairs*

Midway Reprints
Midway Reprints are limited-edition, paper-covered books. The purpose
this series is to keep in print titles for which there is a steady but sm
demand—out-of-print titles, as well as books which might otherwise ha
been declared out of print. In order to keep the prices as low as possib
Midway Reprints will not be issued in clothbound editions.